AF504331

PHONETICS FOR SCOTTISH STUDENTS

PUBLISHED BY

JAMES MACLEHOSE AND SONS, GLASGOW,

Publishers to the University.

MACMILLAN AND CO., LTD., LONDON.

New York,	- -	The Macmillan Co.
Toronto,	- -	The Macmillan Co. of Canada.
London,	- -	Simpkin, Hamilton and Co.
Cambridge,	- -	Bowes and Bowes.
Edinburgh,	- -	Douglas and Foulis.
Sydney,	- -	Angus and Robertson.

MCMIX.

PHONETICS

FOR

SCOTTISH STUDENTS

THE SOUNDS OF POLITE SCOTTISH
DESCRIBED AND COMPARED WITH THOSE OF
POLITE ENGLISH

BY

IRENE F. WILLIAMS, M.A.

LECTURER ON PHONETICS TO THE GLASGOW PROVINCIAL COMMITTEE

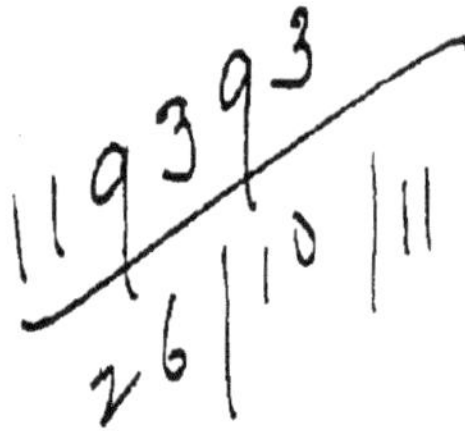

GLASGOW
JAMES MACLEHOSE AND SONS
PUBLISHERS TO THE UNIVERSITY
1909

GLASGOW: PRINTED AT THE UNIVERSITY PRESS
BY ROBERT MACLEHOSE AND CO. LTD.

PREFACE

THE first steps in practical phonetics must be taken from
the standpoint of the student's own sounds. Books on
English phonetics are not useful, they are definitely harmful
to a Scottish beginner ; the spelling conceals existing differences of pronunciation, and the statements of the English
writer misunderstood, disgust and confuse. When the Scottish student has studied his own sounds, and compared and
contrasted them with the English pronunciation, he knows
that great differences exist, and can study English phonetics
with profit from the English standpoint. This book aims
at supplying a link between Scottish students and the
standard phonetic literature. It is with great regret that I
am forced by the exigencies of the case to invent to some
extent my own symbols. When Mr. Daniel Jones' *Pronunciation of English* appeared, with its numerous symbols, I
hoped to be able to adopt them. But it is impossible, for
example, to use eꞮ, iꞮ, uꞮ for the Scottish sounds in *day, queen,
food*; ᴇ, i, u for the English sounds in *red, lip, good*, since
in Scottish the tense sounds are often heard short or half-
long, making it imperatively necessary to have separate
symbols for the tense and slack vowels, to which marks of
length or shortness may be added.

Several of the Scottish extracts are identical with those
given in English in Professor Wyld's *Teaching of Reading*;
this has been done with his consent, to facilitate comparison

of the two dialects. Here again the symbols have been a difficulty. Dealing with Scottish and English, four distinct sounds occur, **o**, *o*, ɔ, ʌ, for each of which a symbol is necessary. In English, where **ou** takes the place of **o**, it is natural to use the symbol **o** for the sound in *not*. Again **a** is needed for the Scottish advanced back sound of *man*, etc., and cannot be used as in English for the sound in *but*. I have found, however, that once students have thoroughly grasped their own sounds and the principles of sound notation, they are able to pass without great difficulty to slightly differing symbols.*

The blank pages are inserted to allow the student to add diagrams from personal observation, and to comment on his individual pronunciation.

I wish to thank Miss Falconer, Miss Sprunt, Mr. Allison, Mr. Renwick, and Mr. Grant of Aberdeen, for preparing, or helping me to prepare the Scottish texts; my students also for aid in various ways always willingly given.

The method of sound-classification adopted is that of Dr. Henry Sweet, to whose writings and teaching my great indebtedness must be obvious to every student of phonetics.

IRENE F. WILLIAMS.

September, 1909.

---

* Before beginning to work at a book with different notation, students should make a list of the new symbols and compare carefully with the old; after reading a few extracts with constant reference to the list, any difficulty ceases.

CONTENTS

I.

AIM AND USE OF PHONETICS.

§ 1. Phonetics is the theory and practice of speech-sounds. The theory can never be understood without practically testing each point as it arises, while on the other hand it is useless to practise sounds unless we know what we are doing.

Every speaker is master of a certain number of sounds, but his control of them is mechanical. He can repeat the sounds in familiar positions, but if asked to isolate them or to alter the position he finds himself in a difficulty. Thus 'wh' in 'why' is easy, but turn the word round and how many speakers will pronounce a final 'wh' correctly? 'ng' in 'king' offers no difficulty, but if we write the word backwards and try to pronounce an initial 'ng,'* we shall find it hard to do so. Vowels, isolated from their normal surroundings, are rarely if ever pronounced correctly by beginners.

Phonetics begins by substituting intelligent for mechanical control in the case of native sounds, and when this is accomplished, proceeds to the acquisition of unfamiliar sounds.

§ 2. Before attempting to reproduce a sound we must hear it correctly. As a rule beginners cannot detect with any

* Note that 'ng' represents one sound only.

A

accuracy the minuter differences of speech-sounds. It is, however, extremely important to be able to do so. From the outset the student should practise listening attentively. To be a good listener is a long step in the direction of becoming a good phonetician.

§ 3. Whether or no phonetics should be taught to children need not be discussed here. That the subject, if properly taught, both interests and amuses them cannot, I think, be denied. Of course, only the simpler sounds should be attempted, and simple language used.

For teachers, phonetics is essential. To their lot falls the task of correcting the pronunciation of the children under their care; and they must be practically conversant with the processes involved in such pronunciation, both the one they wish discarded, and the one they recommend.

§ 4. Unfortunately much ignorance obtains about even the simplest processes of speech. Where children or grown-up people fail to pronounce a certain sound it is usual to describe them as 'defective' speakers, and to accept resignedly their incapacity to pronounce the sound in question.

Now it is only in very rare cases that there is inability to pronounce a sound. Such inability can only exist where there is actual mal-formation or deformity. In the large majority of cases the apparent defect is due to bad habit, not checked in early youth. Speech habits are particularly tyrannous, and a person who has been pronouncing wrongly for years really feels that it is impossible to change.

Improvement is easier and much more effectual in the case of children. It is the duty of every good teacher, therefore, to watch for such cases, one or more of which are found in every large class, to find out exactly what is wrong, and to show the child how he may improve.

In some cases, however, bad speech is due to physical defect; adenoids and a tied tongue being probably the commonest. Here a teacher cannot alter the faulty speech, but may yet help very materially by urging that the slight surgical operations necessary be performed before the speech habits become fixed.

§ 5. Phonetics is also useful to the teachers themselves. They are faced with the difficulty of how to make themselves heard by large classes, and often against contending noise through many hours of each day. Many teachers resort to shouting, and by doing so permanently injure the quality of their voices and lower the standard of discipline. A class where the teacher shouts is always noisy, the children call out their answers at the top of their voices, and move noisily in their desks. Noise is infectious, a fact that young teachers should take to heart.

Nevertheless a teacher must be clearly audible, and how to achieve this is the problem.* Phonetics helps very materially here. Just as in playing the piano, good execution is attained only when each finger has been strengthened by individual exercise, so constant practice of separate sounds helps to a more expert use of the organs of speech. Especially it makes for clearer speech and diminishes the effort of speaking.

§ 6. But phonetics is useful for English-speaking people from quite another point of view. Much ignorance and many false ideas prevail on the subject of pronunciation These arise largely from the fact that our spelling, instead of revealing the actual pronunciation, acts as an effectual disguise. To begin with, the same standard spelling is used by all, no matter how pronunciations may vary. And again, apart from varying pronunciations, English spelling is exceedingly

---

* A few good lessons on voice-production would be useful to those who can obtain them. For some hints on this point compare Wyld, *The Teaching of Reading*, Chap. VI., and Hulbert, *Voice Training in Speech and Song*.

inconsistent in itself, and violates continually the principle
of all good spelling : one sound, one symbol. A prevalent
idea, now happily becoming old-fashioned, was that the
written language was the real language, while spoken language was a more or less unsuccessful attempt to follow the
written. This gave to written words an importance much
beyond their due, and the inconsistencies obviously existing
in spelling led to false ideas about language in general.
The real living language is the spoken language, and true
ideas about it can be gained only by studying actual speech.
Since this inconsistency in spelling has had so much
influence upon men's thoughts about language, it will be
useful to glance back very briefly and see how it arose.

§ 7. Before the Conquest—roughly till about 1100 A.D.—
English was written phonetically. There was no standard
spelling; each scribe represented as faithfully as he could
the sounds he actually pronounced. Hence a manuscript
written by a Kentish scribe varies from one written by a
West Saxon, and still more from one written in the North.

In the middle period (1100-1500) English was still in
intention phonetic, but the French had brought with them a
mode of spelling different from the English one, and the
two continued side by side. This necessarily made for
inconsistency, since so many sounds could now be represented in two ways. Still, throughout this period, the
spelling of any manuscript is a guide to the dialect of
the writer.

When printing was introduced it became necessary to
adopt some one form of spelling. Caxton, although himself
a Kentishman, realised the importance of the London
dialect, and that it was to some extent a mean between the
other dialects. He used its spelling in his press, and it
rapidly became adopted for all printed books.

Between 1500 and 1600 this spelling was altered in

various ways, but since 1600 it has changed only in a few unimportant details.

Meanwhile the spoken language has undergone many important changes, and left the spelling far behind. Looked at in this historical light, we see the absurdity of attempting 'to speak as we spell,' since to do this consistently we must go back to the speech of our forefathers; the necessity, also, of examining the sounds themselves, leaving spelling for the time on one side, if we are to discover how we actually pronounce. For such examination a knowledge of phonetics is essential.

II.

THE TERM "SCOTTISH.

§ 8. The term Scottish is somewhat vaguely used by Englishmen or foreigners to describe the new sounds which meet them North of the Border. As a matter-of-fact there are different kinds and different degrees of Scottish. First of all comes the great distinction between Gaelic and Scottish, two languages exceedingly remote in origin and structure. Then the fact that Scottish itself is not one dialect, but embraces several distinct types, with different sounds, different intonation and so forth. Lastly, there is the Polite Scottish dialect, which is the literary language of England adapted to the Scottish speech basis, or to put it in more popular terms, English spoken with a Scotch accent.

§ 9. Originally the Scot found his home in Ireland, and it was from thence he came, in the seventh and eighth centuries, to settle on the West coast of Alban, above the Clyde.* At this time the Scot was opposed to the Pict, who inhabited the east part of the country above the Forth. In the ninth century a king of Scots became king of the Picts also, and the term Scot was generally applied to all the people dwelling above the Firths. South of the Forth the country was

* For this and following §§ compare Murray, 'The Dialect of the Southern Counties of Scotland,' *Transactions, Philological Society*, 1873.

inhabited by Angles, who had defeated the Britons and settled there soon after their first inroads into Britain.

The Scottish of this period was Gaelic, and it was opposed to 'Inglis,' the Angle dialect spoken south of the Forth, and extending to the Humber.

Ultimately the Lowland Angles came under the political supremacy of the Scottish king, and this marked a turning-point in the history of the monarchy. From now on the king of Scots became more and more closely allied to his powerful Angle subjects, whose language he adopted, and increasingly out of sympathy with the Scottish or Gaelic element. During the twelfth and thirteenth centuries Inglis spread further north along the East coast.

§ 10. The Wars of Independence led to the rise of a definite national feeling in Scotland, and a national hatred of the Southern. The lowlanders felt themselves Scottish as distinct from the English foe, and the term Scotland took the political and geographical significance which it has to-day. Yet to the end of the fifteenth century, the language of Lowland Scotland remained identical with that of Northern England, and both were called 'Inglis.' 'Barbour at Aberdeen and Richard Rolle de Hampole near Doncaster, wrote for their several countrymen in the same identical dialect,' Murray, p. 29, § 12. Further 'John of Fordun (about 1400) speaking of his fellow-countrymen, says :—"For two languages are in use among them—the Scottish and the Teutonic; the people using the latter tongue occupy the sea-coast and lowland districts; the people of Scottish language inhabit the highlands and the isles beyond,"' *ibid*, p. 43, § 14.

§ 11. Towards the end of the fifteenth century the Northern dialect began to develop on individual lines, and from that time on it appropriated more and more consistently the title of Scottish, while the Gaelic tongue was called Ersch.

In England, till about the same period, the three dialects Northern, Midland and Southern stood on an equal footing, and were all three regarded as equally useful for literary purposes.   Now the Midland dialect became the standard spoken dialect and the sole language of literature.   Between this form of English and the Inglis of Scotland there were very real differences, and hence it became natural to speak of the Inglis of Scotland as Scottish.

§ 12. Between the fifteenth and early seventeenth centuries Scotland developed, as a medium for a flourishing literature, a literary dialect much influenced by French.   This dialect was used with remarkable uniformity by all writers of this period.*   It was, and remained, however, a literary language, and the many foreign elements which characterise it left no permanent traces on the spoken dialects.

§ 13. The influence of the Reformation drew Scotland into closer touch with England.   There was no Scottish Bible, and the use of the English version in Scotland familiarised all classes with the standard English speech.   The importance of this fact can hardly be overestimated.

§ 14. The Union of the Crowns under James VI. gave its death-blow to Scottish as a literary language, but the spoken dialects continued as before.   To-day they are dying out, thrust into the background by education, ease of transit, books, newspapers and so forth, and their place is taken by the dialect which we have called Polite Scottish.   The children come to the schools speaking broad Scots and gradually acquire the standard form.†   The original dialect is not usually entirely abandoned.   It is kept for intimate home use or for moments of emotion or excitement.

* Cp. Smith, *Specimens of Middle Scots*, p. xii.

† For a similar observation cp. Mutschmann, *A Phonology of the North-Eastern Dialect*, Bonn Diss., 1909, § 7.

§15. Polite Scottish is English adapted to the speaker's natural speech tendencies. These tendencies vary in different parts of Scotland, so that Polite Scottish is not itself entirely uniform.

Throughout this book the term Scottish is used to denote that form of Polite Scottish heard from educated speakers in the South-West of Scotland.

III.

OBSERVATION OF THE ORGANS OF SPEECH.

§ 16. Let us ask ourselves at the outset what is the *material* out of which speech-sounds are made?   Utter quite naturally some simple sentence—'fingers were made before forks'—and look all the while at your reflexion in a small glass. The lips move, sometimes meeting each other, sometimes the teeth. So much is easily seen. Now ask yourself: What is the material which these movements are manipulating, what is it that escapes between the lips? It is the breath, of course, and if you hold your breath, though you make exactly the same lip movements, no speech will result.

Breath, then, is the raw material out of which, by various and intricate movements, speech is made.

§ 17. Our next task is to discover what tools we have at our disposal for shaping the raw material. These tools are usually called the speech-organs. Pronounce aloud and distinctly the initial sounds * in *by* and *vain*. With what organs is the breath manipulated to form these sounds?†   In *b* both lips are at work, in *v* the lower lip is placed against the upper teeth. The organs thus discovered are—**Lips**, upper and lower, and the **Upper Teeth**.

* Not the name of the initial letter, which itself consists of two sounds.

†My questions presuppose that the reader has a glass, and refers to it before attempting an answer.

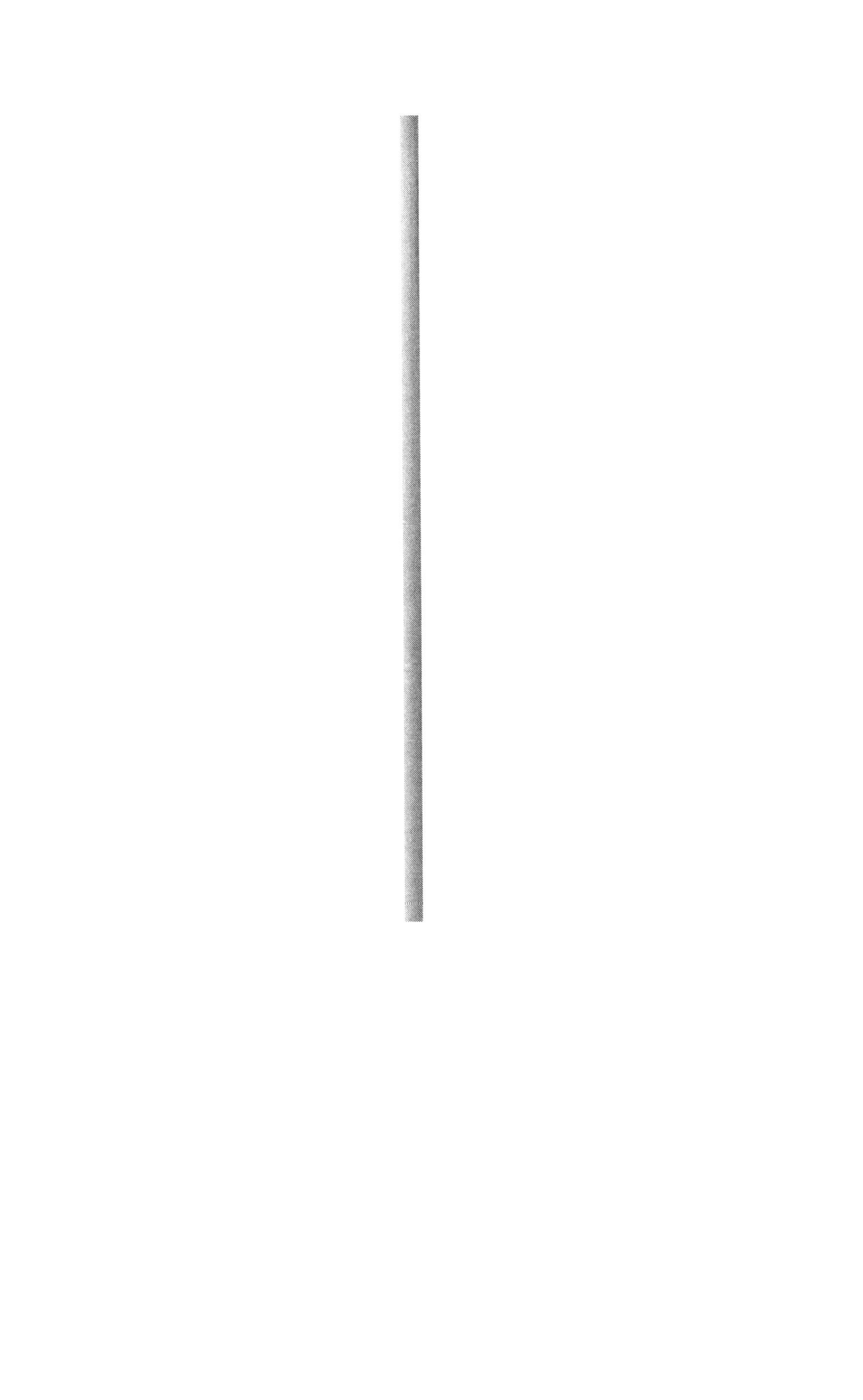

§ 18. Now pronounce *they*, and afterwards isolate the con-sonant *th*.* The movement can be easily seen and felt. The tongue is pushed forwards, and either touches the upper teeth or is placed between the teeth. Add the **Tongue** and the **Lower Teeth** to our list of tools.

§ 19. The tongue is so important in speech, and is used in so many different ways, that we must distinguish between different parts of it. In *they* we see that the foremost part, the tip or point, comes forward to the teeth, but in *caw* this is not the case, and yet we are conscious that the tongue moves. Isolate the initial sound in *caw*. If we look well into the mouth we see that the back part of the tongue rises. Now pronounce *y*, as in *ye*, and then, one after the other, *caw, ye, they*. For the initial sound of *caw* the back part of the tongue moves, for *th* in *they* the point moves, but for *y* in *ye* it is the middle part which is active. For the present it is sufficient to distinguish these three parts of the tongue —**Back, Middle**† and **Point**.

§ 20. Now just as the part of the tongue which articulates varies, so also the opposing organ, or organ against which a sound is made, is not always the same. Pronounce again the three initial sounds of *caw, ye* and *they* respectively, and consider in each case the nature of the opposing organ. In the first the back of the tongue presses on the soft palate, in the second the middle is near the hard palate, and in the third the point is on the teeth. Add to the organs of speech the **Soft** and **Hard Palates.**‡

§ 21. Between the hard palate and the teeth there is another organ which is very important in English speech. If we utter the words *ten, den, Ned, read, Nell* we find that in all

---

* How many sounds are represented by the *th* in *they*?

† Another name for Middle is Front.

‡ By running the finger backwards along the hard palate and so on to the soft palate the difference between the two may be distinctly felt.

the consonants the tongue is well forward in the mouth, but still not on the teeth. First make quite sure where the tongue is by repeating these words, and then put your finger in your mouth and feel the nature of the organ. It is an arch or ridge with a rough, honey-combed surface, just above and behind the upper teeth, called **the Teeth-ridge.**

§ 22. Pronounce now the word *am*, dwelling on the latter sound and ultimately pronouncing it alone and with emphasis. How does it differ from the sounds we have been discussing? Compare *m* and *b*; in both the lips are closed, but whereas in *b* the lips are quickly opened to allow the breath to pass out (put your hand to your lips and you will feel this), in *m* the lips continue closed How is it possible then for the sound to be uttered? The answer is easily discovered—the breath is passing through the nose. We must add the **Nose** then to our lists of tools.

§ 23. We have now discovered the following organs: Lips ; Teeth ; Back, Middle and Point of Tongue ; Soft and Hard Palates ; Teeth-ridge ; Nose.

IV.

THE ORGANS OF SPEECH.

§ 24. The aim of the last lesson was to discover, by observation and experiment, some of the organs of speech. We will now follow the air-stream systematically and see what changes it undergoes.

Air is breathed in* and stored in the **Lungs**; as it passes out again it undergoes the various processes which turn it into speech.

In ordinary breathing, the muscular action is independent of will, but in speaking, and especially in reading aloud, or speaking before an audience, we must exercise conscious control. Sufficient breath must be taken in the pauses caused naturally by the subject, to carry one over to the next similar pause. Breathing must never be allowed to interrupt the sense.

§ 25. From the lungs the breath passes up the **Windpipe**, which widens at its upper end into the **Larynx**. The larynx or Adam's apple can be distinctly felt and in some cases seen. It is of the first importance in speech.

§ 26. **Function of the Larynx.** All breath must pass through the larynx in its way from the lungs to the mouth or nose. Inside the larynx are the **Voice-Curtains**, which

---

* Certain nature sounds, as distinct from speech, are made on the intake of the breath. Thus, a breath sharply drawn in between lower lip and upper teeth expresses sudden, sharp pain, and so on.

are made of thin, elastic membrane, and are capable of being drawn together, so that they close the exit from the windpipe ; or drawn back, so that this exit is free and open. Thus, when the curtains close, the windpipe has a thin elastic covering, formed of two curtains meeting in the middle, otherwise the top of the windpipe is uncovered.

In ordinary breathing the curtains are far apart, and the breath escapes silently into the nose, but in speech the curtains are constantly moving backwards and forwards, and the breath can no longer escape silently.

§ 27. **Movements of Voice-Bands and their effect on Speech.**

(1) The case where the curtains are drawn together, and the windpipe has a thin, elastic covering.

The breath coming up the windpipe finds its way impeded, and there ensues something which may be described as a struggle between the escaping breath and the muscles which keep the voice-bands drawn across the passage. The delicate membranes cannot keep the breath back altogether, except by a great effort of the controlling muscles. The breath escapes in little puffs between the curtains, but after each such escape the muscles bring the curtains together again.

This forcing of the breath between the drawn voice-curtains makes the curtains quiver and vibrate, and this vibration gives to the escaping air the quality known as **Voice.**

(2) The case where the curtains are apart, and the exit from the windpipe has no covering. The air coming from the lungs passes through the larynx unchecked (precisely as if the voice-curtains were non-existent), and therefore silently. This silent passage through the open curtains is what is known in phonetics as **Breath.**

(3) There is a third case where the curtains are partially

drawn (cp. § 29). Room is allowed for the breath to escape, but not silently. It rubs against the half-open curtains, and the rubbing or frictional sound can be clearly heard. This is called **Whisper.**

§ 28. **Formation of the Larynx.** The larynx is a three-cornered box made of cartilage (gristle) and muscle. It is so contrived that, firstly, it protects the delicate voice-curtains, and secondly, it provides by movements of both muscle and cartilage for the stretching and relaxing of the curtains. The outer walls of the box are formed by two cartilages : the **Thyroid** and the **Cricoid.**

The Thyroid consists of two wing-shaped cartilages, joined together in front but open at the back. The ridge where they join in front can be distinctly felt. This supplies the front and the two side walls of the box.

By placing the two hands together at an angle so that the sides, just below the little fingers, touch, while the thumbs are fairly wide apart, some idea of the shape may be gained. The junction of the hands corresponds to the front wall of the larynx, the hands sloping from this angle are the two side walls.

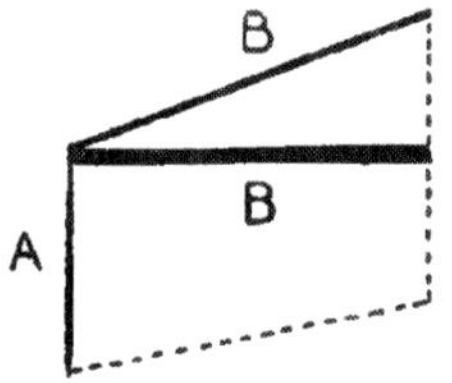

Fig. 1.—**A** = Front wall. **B** = Side wall.

The Cricoid is often called the ring-cartilage, because it has some resemblance to a seal ring. It is placed under the thyroid in front, but at the back, where the thyroid opens, the part resembling a seal rises up and forms the back wall of the voice-box.

This may be illustrated roughly by placing a broad elastic band round the two wrists, keeping the hands in the position already suggested. This indicates the cricoid in front. A watch held between the bases of the thumbs will represent the back wall. Hold the watch in such a position that the glass faces towards the angle made by the fingers.

§ 29. **Arrangement of the Voice-Curtains in the Larynx.** In front the voice-curtains are joined together and fixed at the angle where the thyroid cartilages meet. Their various movements are directed from the other end, or back wall of the box. Here we have to do with two other cartilages which are of the first importance owing to their extraordinary capacity for movement. These are the **Aretenoid** or Pyramid cartilages.

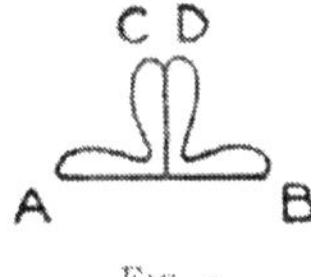

FIG. 2.

Their lower surfaces, A, B, rest on the seal part of the ring-cartilage. The rounded ends C, D turn inwards towards the angle of the thyroid, and to each of these a voice-curtain is attached.

As the aretenoids move they draw the voice-bands after them. The following diagrams illustrate the chief positions found in speech.*

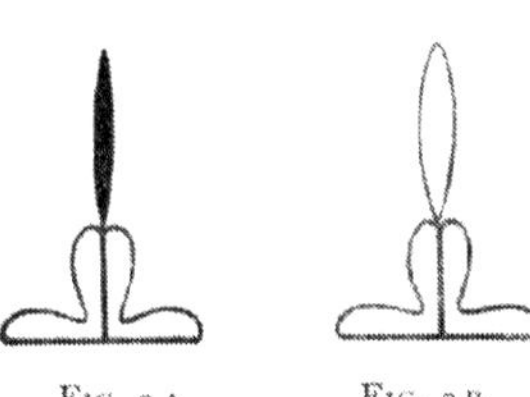

FIG. 3 A.　　FIG. 3 B.

Voice-curtains closed and opening resulting in Voice.

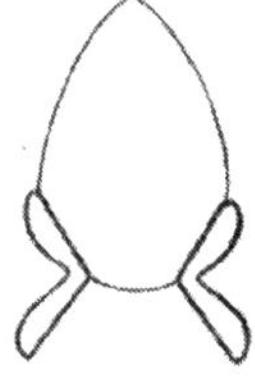

FIG. 4.

Voice-curtains wide apart resulting in Breath.

* See Jespersen, *Lehrbuch d. Phonetik*, from which the suggestion for these diagrams is taken.

Diagrams 5 and 6 represent two degrees of Whisper—
'strong' and 'weak' (cp. Sweet, *Primer of Phonetics*[3], § 27).

Fig. 5.   Fig. 6.*

In strong whisper the bands meet and allow no breath to
pass through, but the air escapes between the aretenoids.
This is the most usual case.

In weak whisper the bands and the aretenoids together
form a narrow passage for the air.

§ 30. Above the larynx, and at the back of the mouth
and nose, is the **Pharynx** or throat. The back wall of this
cavity may be distinctly seen, if the student says 'ah' and
holds the mouth wide open.

§ 31. The breath must pass through larynx and pharynx,
but afterwards there is a choice of passages: it may finally
escape through the **Mouth** or through the **Nose.** The
organ which regulates this escape is the movable **Soft
Palate**, which can be lifted upwards and backwards or
lowered, so that it comes down over the back of the
tongue. The **Uvula** is attached to the soft palate, and
moves with it.

The movement of the soft palate and uvula can be clearly
seen, and should be carefully observed. Say the final
consonant in *rang*,* opening the mouth widely, and notice
that the soft palate seems to fold down over the back of the
tongue. Now say 'ah,' and observe three things: (1) the
tensity of the soft palate, (2) the changed position of

* ng represents only one sound.

the palate and uvula, (3) that under and beyond them one sees the back wall of the throat. These movements of the soft palate and the consequent alteration in the direction of the air-stream are at the root of the distinction between nasal and oral sounds.

§ 32. In nasal sounds the soft palate hangs down, completely blocking the way into the mouth, and the breath passes over it into the nose.

In oral sounds the lifted palate blocks the way from the throat to the nose, but leaves the passage into the mouth wide open. The breath passes under the palate into the mouth.

§ 33. In the nose the breath undergoes no further modification beyond acquiring nasality, but in the mouth it may be manipulated in many ways, owing to the numerous organs found there.

§ 34. We can now trace the air-stream from the lungs outward to the outer air, and in so doing recapitulate all the organs of speech :

The air leaves the lungs, passes up the windpipe and into the larynx. Here it forces its way through closed curtains (Voice), or passes freely and silently through open curtains (Breath) into the throat. If the soft palate is down, the breath or voice passes above it through the open door into the nose, and so into the outer air. If the soft palate is raised, the breath or voice passes under it into the mouth. Here the following organs await it, and help in its manipulation : the tongue, back, middle and point ; the uvula ; the palates, soft and hard ; the teeth-ridge ; the teeth ; the lips.

V.

THE SOUNDS OF SPEECH.

§ 35. The sounds of speech may be divided into two great groups—vowels and consonants.

Before discussing either group in detail we must decide how they differ.

Compare the following four sounds, *a* (as in f*a*ther), *i* (as in mar*i*ne), *z* (as in *z*oo), *d* (as in *d*en).   In

    a the air-passage in the mouth is wide ;

    i the air-passage in the mouth is narrow ;

    z the air-passage in the mouth is narrow ;

    d the air-passage in the mouth is totally closed and then abruptly opened.

Now, obviously *a* and *d* are quite distinct, the one from the other, since in one the air-passage is very wide, and in the other totally closed ; but the distinction between *i* and *z* is less clear. The air-passage through the mouth is narrow for both, and at first it is not easy to see what it is that makes one a vowel and the other a consonant. The distinction between them lies in the *degree* of narrowing of the air-passage. In *i* the passage through the mouth is narrow, but it is just sufficiently large to allow the breath to escape without audibly rubbing on the sides of the passage. In *z* the passage through the mouth has been so far narrowed that the breath has to rub audibly against the passage walls.

It is the presence or absence of audible friction in the mouth which decides whether any given sound is consonant or vowel.

§ 36. For Vowels the air-passage in the mouth may be wide (as in *a*) or narrow (as in *i*), but it must never be so narrow that the breath in its escape causes audible friction.

For Consonants the air-passage in the mouth is either a very narrow one, so that the escaping breath rubs along the passage walls and causes audible friction (*z*), or it is totally closed and then abruptly opened (*d*).

§ 37. To these definitions we may add the following difference : Vowels are all Voiced ; * Consonants are either Voiced or Breathed.

§ 38. We may now turn to the classification of these two groups of sounds. The consonants are much the easier to grasp, and will therefore be discussed first.

---

* This is not universally true, cp. the frequent unvoicing of vowel sounds in French.

VI.

CLASSIFICATION OF CONSONANTS.

§ 39. DEFINITION. Consonants are either Voice or Breath, accompanied by audible friction or total stoppage in the mouth (cp. §§ 36, 37).

§ 40. The Classification of Consonants * depends upon four points.

1. The position of the Voice-Bands in the Larynx.

2. The position of the Soft Palate and Uvula.

3. The shape and size of the air-passage in the mouth.

4. The place of articulation in the mouth.

1. **The position of the Voice-Bands in the Larynx.** This divides all consonants into two groups. Group I., Voice Consonants, in which the voice-bands are stretched and vibrating (cp. § 27). Ex. **b**,† **v**, **z**, etc. Group II., Breath Consonants, in which the voice-bands are relaxed and the breath passes freely through the larynx (cp. § 27). Ex. **p**, **f**, **s**, etc.

---

*The aim of classification is obviously to group together all the sounds which are similarly articulated, and to separate those which differ. Before reading this chapter, the student should note down all his consonants and try to group them for himself.

† Black print indicates that the sound, not the name of the letter or letters, is meant, and that it is to be pronounced aloud.

2. **The position of the Soft Palate and Uvula.** Group I., Nasal Consonants, where the soft palate is lowered and the breath escapes through the nose. Ex. **m, n,** etc. Group II., Oral or Mouth Consonants, where the soft palate is drawn upwards and backwards, and the breath escapes under it into the mouth. Ex. **k, g, l,** etc.

3. **The shape and size of the air-passage in the mouth.**

CASE I. **Stop** consonants. Ex. **d, b.** The air-passage in the mouth is completely blocked for a moment and the air is kept back, then the way is opened and the air comes out in a puff.* These sounds cannot be prolonged.

CASE II. **Continuant** or **Open** consonants. Ex. **s, v, f.** The air-passage in the mouth is very narrow, and the air has to press through, rubbing as it does so, on either side of the passage. It escapes in a regular stream, and the sound can be prolonged at will.

CASE III. **Divided** or **Side** consonants. Ex. **l.** The air-passage in the mouth is divided, the centre part being closed, the two sides left open. The air escapes at the sides in two † uninterrupted streams, and the sound can be prolonged at will.

CASE IV. **Nasal** consonants. Ex. **m, n.** The air-passage in the mouth is stopped completely. The air escapes through the nose (cp. 2), in a regular stream and the sound can be prolonged at will.

CASE V. **Trilled** consonants. Ex. **r** (Scottish pronunciation). Some flexible body—uvula, tip of tongue or lips—is placed in the way of a strong current of air through the mouth, and for a moment checks it. The air pushes away this impediment, which however immediately reinstates

---

* This puff of breath is called the off-glide of the stop consonant. (Cp. Sweet, *Primer of Phonetics*, p. 55.)

† Sometimes the breath escapes at one side only, hence 'side' consonant is perhaps the better name.

itself. According as this is done, once or often, we have a single or a prolonged trill.

4 **The place of articulation in the mouth.**

(i) **Back** consonants are made between the back of the tongue and the soft palate. Ex. **k.**

(ii) **Middle** consonants, between the middle of the tongue and the hard palate. Ex. **y** as in *yet.*

(iii) **Point** consonants, between the point of the tongue and the teeth-ridge. Ex. **d.**

(iv) **Blade** * consonants, between the blade of the tongue and the hard palate. Ex. **s** as in *see.*

(v) **Blade-Point.** The whole tongue is drawn somewhat backwards from the Blade position, and the Point is raised and shares in the articulation of the consonant The opposing organs are Hard Palate and Teeth-ridge. Ex. **sh,** as in *short.*

(vi) **Point-Teeth** consonants are made between the tip of the tongue and the upper teeth. Ex. **th,** in *then.*

(vii) **Lip-Teeth** consonants, between the lower lip and the upper teeth. Ex. **v**

(viii) **Lip** consonants are made when the two lips are brought together. Ex. **b.**

(ix) **Lip-back.** The Back of the tongue is raised towards the Soft Palate, and at the same time the Lips are brought forward. Ex. **w.**

NOTE 1 Note that where only one word is used to describe a group of consonants, as for example Back, Middle, Point, the term refers to the moving organ (the organ which moves to make the sound). Where two words are used, the second does not always refer to the same thing. Thus in Point-teeth, Lip-teeth, the second term refers in each case to the opposing organ; but in Blade-Point, Lip-Back, the

---

* The blade is not a separate part of the tongue, but a different way of using it. When the tongue is broadened and flattened, the part immediately behind the point is called the blade.

second term refers to the movement of an additional organ, or another part of the same organ.

NOTE 2. The Lip-Back consonants differ from all other English consonants in being made by the simultaneous action of two independent organs in the mouth, the tongue and the lips. Consonants so made are described as Modified Consonants.

§ 41. By combining the points just considered we arrive at the following method of tabulating consonants :

Consonant Table.

		Back.	Middle.	Point.	Blade.	Blade-Point.	Point-Teeth.	Lip.	Lip-Teeth.	Lip-Back.
Voiced.	Stop, -	g								
	Open, -									w
	Divided,									
	Nasal, -									
	Trill, -									
Breathed.	Stop, -									
	Open, -									M
	Divided,									
	Nasal, -									
	Trill, -									

VII.

CONSONANTS OF SCOTTISH.

§42. We must now consider individually the consonants of our normal speech, and find out where each should be placed on the table.

Isolate the initial consonants of each of the following words: *but* **b**, *pot* **p**, *met* **m**.

Is there any characteristic shared in common by all three sounds? Obviously there is: both lips are used in all three cases. They belong then to the Lip column of the table (cp. p. 23 (viii)).

The precise place of each has next to be decided   **b** and **p** are both stops (cp. p. 22) but they must be placed in different squares, since **b** is voiced, **p** breathed.   **m** like **b** is voiced, but must be placed on the table as a nasal, since to form it the breath passes through the nose (cp. p. 22).*

§43. Take next the initials of *vie* and *fie*: **v** and **f**. Repeat the two sounds and make quite sure of the exact process of formation by watching your mouth in a mirror. The lower lip is brought against the lower edge of the upper teeth and held there firmly, meanwhile the breath is expelled through the spaces between the upper teeth. The degree of firmness is somewhat greater for **v** than for **f**. Since both sounds are made by the junction of lip and teeth they are

---

* The reader should make a consonant table and fill in each sound for himself.

both to be placed in the lip-teeth column. To which square does each belong? Repeat the sounds again and try to prolong them. This is easily done if we have a good supply of breath, for the way of the air-stream is open, nothing blocks its passage. Both **v** and **f** are open or continuant consonants (cp. p. 22), but they belong to different squares, since **v** is voiced, while **f** is breathed.

§ 44. The next sounds are the initials of *then* and *thin*, in which, again, the formation is very easily observed. Repetition of these two sounds and comparison with the foregoing shows that we have passed away from the lip columns and come to sounds in which the tongue is the active organ. First, what part of the tongue moves, and secondly, what is the organ towards which it moves? We can both see and feel that it is the tip or point of the tongue which moves, and that it is placed either behind the upper teeth or between the two rows of teeth. These two sounds are point-teeth consonants (cp. p. 23 (vi)); a little examination will show that both are open or continuant, and that the initial consonant of *then* is voiced while that of *thin* is voiceless.

It is convenient to have a symbol for each of these sounds before inserting them in the table. Voiced *th* as in *then*, *other*, etc. is written ð, voiceless or breathed *th* as in *thin*, *author* is written þ.

§ 45. Take next the following group of sounds : **d** in *den*, **l** in *led*, **n** in *Nell*, **t** in *tell*.

It is important to consider these here, because, while some of my readers will find these to form a group of sounds agreeing together and differing from the previous group, others may find that in their pronunciation two at least of the sounds here mentioned, namely, **d** and **t**, should rather be placed with the foregoing as point-teeth consonants. Each reader should be careful to see that on his own consonant table his sounds appear as he makes them, and not in imitation of any book.

As in the case of the foregoing sounds, it is the point of the tongue which moves, but whereas in ð the point comes

on to the upper teeth. in **d, t, n,** 1 the point comes in contact
with the arch above and behind the upper teeth, called the
teeth-ridge (cp § 2 1) All these sounds belong, in the speech
of the majority, to the point column. I have, however,
come across more than one case where **d** and **t,** especially
before **r,** were articulated between the point of the tongue
and the teeth and belonged therefore not to the point but
to the point-teeth column.

It will be easy to place these sounds, each in its right square.
In **d** and **t** the breath's passage is first totally blocked, then
suddenly opened , these sounds are therefore stopped consonants : in n the breath escapes through the nose, and in 1
the air-passage through the mouth is divided (cp. p. 22,
Case III.). **d, n,** 1 agree in being voiced, **t** is voiceless

§ 46 The point consonants are not yet exhausted The
consonant *r* remains. It is a common misconception to
regard all *r*-sounds as trills. Students will describe each
sound in a word in detail until they come to an *r* which
they dismiss without further remark as 'a trill.' This is
open to objection on two sides; firstly, the sound is very
often not a trill at all, and secondly, if it be so, that fact
does not exhaust the information which must be given about
it. Notice first then that there are two possibilities in
pronouncing *r*: (1) it may be pronounced as an open
consonant, (2) it may be trilled

In forming the open *r* (phonetic symbol ɹ) the tip of the
tongue is raised to the teeth-ridge and held there, a small
passage is left between the centre part of the tongue and the
centre part of the ridge, and through this the breath passes
out in a steady stream In the trilled **r** the process is
different. The tip is raised against the ridge, but is instantly
pushed down by a strong current of air from the lungs;
it reinstates itself by means of its muscular force, only to be
again thrust down. In a strong trill this happens often.

The commonest form of **r** in the North is a slight trill; stronger trills are heard in excited or emphatic speech. The untrilled ɪ occurs much more frequently than is generally imagined.

In addition to these two point *r*-sounds, the back *r* is frequently heard from individual speakers. Those who pronounce this sound are often not aware that they are substituting one form of *r* for another, but they do realise that they fail to pronounce the normal sound. The back *r*-sound will be discussed together with other back consonants in the following paragraph.

§ 47. Pronounce aloud the consonants in the following words: *go, king, loch.* Of these, one sound, l, which we have had already and found to be point divided (§ 45), may be eliminated. Notice that the digraphs *ng, ch* represent one sound only in each case; their phonetic symbols are respectively ŋ and χ. What characteristic have these four sounds in common : **g, k,** ŋ, χ ? If we repeat them aloud and concentrate our attention on the movements of the speech organs * we shall discover that they are all alike made by the back of the tongue in conjunction with the soft palate. Take the sound **g** : here the back part of the tongue is placed firmly against the soft palate, so that the breath is kept back altogether, then the tongue moves down again and the breath escapes. The formation of **k** in the mouth is exactly similar. Both are back stop consonants, but they differ as regards voicing ; **g** is voiced, **k** is breathed.

In ŋ the tongue is again against the soft palate and remains there, the voice escaping meanwhile through the nose. In χ, as in *loch,* a small passage is left between the back of the tongue and the soft palate, and by this means the breath passes out uninterrupted.

To return to the back *r* referred to in § 46. Many of

* It is often helpful to shut one's eyes.

those who use it would be glad to get rid of it and to pronounce instead the point sound In substituting one sound for another the best means is as follows: find out all about the sound you pronounce, what organs move, how they move, and so on. You will then know what to avoid; secondly find out all about the sound you wish to acquire, and bring all your patience to bear on trying to move the organs in the new way. Omit the sound altogether rather than pronounce in the old way. A few days of constant practice will be more useful than weeks or even years of occasional attempts at the new, while still generally pronouncing the old.

How then is this back *r*-sound made? Often it is a voiced, back, open consonant—the sound χ pronounced with voice. Sometimes the uvula trills slightly. In either case the back of the tongue is raised, and this is what must be avoided. In the sound which we wish to substitute, the tip must be raised. Speakers who have this sound find it at first impossible to make any *r* at all with the tip of the tongue. The best method to pursue is to go over and over the other point sounds to strengthen the control over this part of the tongue. Next put the point very near the ridge, and try to make an *r*-sound in this position. If the student can once realise the point *r* position the battle is half won. After that it is only a matter of strengthening his conception by constant practice, and refusing to pronounce the old sound. This change is undoubtedly extremely difficult for grown-up speakers; all the more incumbent is it upon teachers to make sure that the children under their care pronounce *r* correctly *

---

* Avoid teasing children to trill *r* very loudly or even at all. If they pronounce a clear point open it is quite sufficient. I have met with cases where harm had been done by this effort to get an exaggerated trill

§ 48. Take next the initial sound in *you*, *yes*, and the finals of *dreich* and *skreich*.

There is sometimes a difficulty in realising that the name of the letter *u* consists of two sounds, and this is the first point to make sure of.   The word *mew*, for instance, has three sounds, the second being the same consonant which occurs initial in *yes*.   How is this sound made?   Compare the *y*-sound (written **j** in phonetics) with the sound **g**.   **g** we know is made between the back of the tongue and the soft palate.   **j** differs in both points; it is made between the middle of the tongue and the hard palate.   It is therefore a middle consonant, and must be placed in that column. It is voiced, and is a kind of open consonant, though not naturally a continuant (cp. *w* § 51).

Further, compare **j** in *yes*, etc., with ð, **d**.   Notice that whereas in the latter sounds the point of the tongue turns up (in ð against the upper teeth, in **d** against the teeth ridge) in **j** the point is at the base of the lower teeth.   This should be kept in mind in any attempt to acquire other middle sounds.   The sound heard in *dreich, skreich* (phonetic symbol ç) is made by placing the tongue in a position similar to that necessary for **j**, and unvoicing.   It is the voiceless, open, middle consonant.

Note that between the back sound χ as in *loch*, and the true middle ç, many intermediate shades are possible, just as the **k** heard in *cart* and that heard in *king* are not identical, the latter being made further forward in the mouth than the former.   In *Brechin* the *ch* generally represents a sound somewhat retracted from the middle position, whereas *ch* in *Ecclefechan* has a back open sound advanced.

ç is heard as a glide * between **t** and **j** in some pro-

---

* A glide is a slight indefinite sound made as the organs pass from one position to another (see Sweet, *Primer of Phonetics*, pp. 52-64, and cp. p. 22, Case I. and note).

nunciations of *nature*, etc., and it occurs initially in *Hugh*, etc.

§49. Isolate the initial sounds of *see* and *zoo*, and the finals of *this* and *is*. Note that the letter *s* does not always indicate the same sound. In phonetics **s** is the symbol for the sound in *see*, *this*, **z** for the sound in *is* and *zoo*.

In forming these sounds the blade of the tongue is used, and we should try to realise first of all what the blade is. Compare þ with **s**. In þ the point is elongated, in **s** the whole fore part is broadened and flattened. When the tongue has this broad, flat shape, the part immediately behind the tip (not so far back as the middle) is used to form the sounds in question and is called the blade (cp. p. 23 (iv)).

By repeating the sounds **s, z,** again, we may also discover that the opposing organ is the teeth-ridge. Both sounds can be prolonged, and are therefore continuants ; **z** is voiced, **s** voiceless.

§50. Pass now to two other sounds closely related to the preceding : *sh* in *she, hush,* and the sound represented by *s* in *measure*, and by *z* in *azure*. The symbols for these two sounds are respectively ʃ and ʒ ('long-tailed *s* and *z*'). The first point to note is, that while in **s, z,** the point of the tongue is inactive, in ʃ, ʒ it is raised, and shares with the blade the task of making the two sounds. Hence these sounds are called Blade-Point consonants.

Further, if we compare **s** with ʃ. we find that in the latter sound the whole tongue is drawn somewhat back from the **s** position ; the blade functions against the hard palate, and the point is opposite the teeth-ridge. The shape of the tongue, too, varies somewhat. In **s, z,** the breath passes over the wide, flat tongue ; in ʃ, ʒ, the tongue is somewhat hollowed in the centre all along the blade and point, and the air passes through this central narrow hollowing or channel.

D

It will be easily recognised that ʒ is open or continuant voiced, and ʃ open or continuant voiceless.

§51. The initial sounds of *was, what*, are interesting, since they are formed by the simultaneous action of two sets of organs. Such consonants are known as 'modified' consonants (cp. p. 24, Note 2); *w* and *wh* (phonetic symbol ʍ) are the only instances of such sounds in our language. It is easy to see that the lips move to form these sounds, but the other organs are less easily discovered. Pronounce the vowel **u** (not its name, but its sound, as in *who*). Ignore the lip movement and concentrate on the tongue; then try to answer the question: Where is the back of the tongue? It will be found that the back of the tongue is quite close to the soft palate, and exactly the same is true in the case of **w** and ʍ. These sounds are made by moving the lips forward and by raising the back of the tongue to the soft palate. They are called *Lip-back* consonants, 'back' referring to the part of the tongue used.

It is obvious that **w** is voiced and ʍ voiceless, but are they open sounds or stops? If we compare **w**, ʍ with **s** or **f** we are struck at once by differences. In **w**, ʍ the organs move during the enunciation of the sound, and the sensation rather resembles that felt in forming a stop (for ex. **d**) than a continuant, such as **s**. Again, **w**, ʍ end like stops in a puff of breath which cannot be prolonged. The first part of the sound can be prolonged, but not with the naturalness which characterises all true continuants. Nevertheless, though not continuants in the true sense, these sounds must be classed as open consonants, since in making them the outward passage of the breath is never completely stopped. They are best described as *Moving Open* consonants, and as such are to be distinguished from *Continuant Open* consonants. **j** is the only other of our consonants belonging to this class (cp. § 48).

§ 52. In all the sounds examined the consonantal friction or stoppage took place in the mouth. It has not been so much as suggested that consonants could be made in any other way.* We must now examine two sounds in which the friction or stoppage is not in the mouth.

I. Pronounce aloud *had, hot, heat,* and isolate and prolong the initial consonant. How is it made? A few repetitions will suggest that the sound is breath with some stress upon it. Where is its consonantal friction, since it is not in the mouth? Repeat the sounds and try to find this out. The breath is rubbing on the voice-curtains, which are partly opened, and the friction is caused there. The opening between the voice-curtains is called the **Glottis**, so we may describe **h** as a *Glottal Continuant.* If you find this in the least degree confusing you may think of **h** and describe it as *Stressed Breath.*

You will have noticed that **h** varies according to the vowel that follows. This depends upon the fact that **h** itself has no consonantal position in the mouth; the organs are free to prepare for the following vowel, and hence the stressed breath, **h,** passes now through one shape of mouth channel, now through another, and varies with each.

II. The second sound is not generally recognised as belonging to Polite Scottish, but you may have heard it, as I have done, from uneducated people, in whose speech it takes the place of the **t**-sound in *water, butter,* etc. Perhaps you can imitate this sound fairly successfully; if so, please do so, as I would like you to realise how it is made.

What happens is this: Instead of moving the tongue upwards to the teeth-ridge, and forming a stop consonant in the mouth, the speaker makes a stop in the larynx. During the enunciation of the two vowel sounds in *water,* etc., the voice-curtains are close together and vibrating; after the

* To avoid confusion which otherwise invariably arises.

first vowel and before the second the curtains are drawn so tightly that they cease to vibrate, and entirely stop the passage of the breath (cp. §27); this leads to an instant's silence, after which the bands vibrate again and the second vowel is heard. In formation this corresponds exactly to an oral stop, **d**, **b**, etc., only that instead of the tongue meeting the roof of the mouth, or the lips being closed, it is the voice-curtains which first keep the breath back and then release it. This sound is called a Glottal Stop, and its symbol is **ʔ**

In Polite Scottish this sound often occurs before initial vowels when it has the effect of making the vowel more distinct (compare the regular occurrence of this sound in a slightly stronger form before initial vowels in German, and the 'attack' necessary for vowels in good singing).

§ 53. Table of Scottish Consonants.

		Back.	Middle.	Point.	Blade.	Blade-Point.	Point-Teeth.	Lip.	Lip-Teeth.	Lip-Back.
Voiced.	Stop, -	g		d				b		
	Open, -		j	ɹ	z	ʒ	ð		v	w
	Divided,			l						
	Nasal, -	ŋ		n				m		
	Trill, -	(ʀ)		r						
Breathed.	Stop, -	k		t				p		
	Open, -	χ	ç		s	ʃ	þ		f	ʍ
	Divided,									
	Nasal, -									
	Trill, -									

Stressed Breath **h.**　　　　Glottal Stop **ʔ**

VIII.

CLASSIFICATION OF VOWELS.

§ 54. DEFINITION. A normal vowel is Voice without audible friction or stoppage in the mouth.

§ 55. The most important factor in the formation of vowels is the tongue, which is divided for vowel classification into two parts only, called respectively the *Back* and the *Front*.

The nature of any vowel is decided by consideration of the following points :

 (1) What part of the tongue articulates.
 (2) The distance between that part and the roof of the mouth.
 (3) The condition of the muscles of the tongue.
 (4) The movements of the lips.

§ 56. (1) **What part of the tongue articulates.** A vowel may be made either with the Back or the Front of the tongue; such vowels are called respectively **Back** and **Front** vowels. The vowel sound in *zoo* is a Back vowel; the vowel in *see* is a Front vowel. In *oo* the back of the tongue is raised towards the soft palate, and the rest of the tongue slopes downwards from the back of the mouth to the front. In *ee* the slope is in the opposite direction. The front of the tongue is raised towards the hard palate, and the rest of the tongue slopes downwards, from front to back. Both

Front and Back vowels may be included under the name of 'sloped' vowels.

There is a third class of vowels, called **Flat** vowels. In these there is no slope; the tongue is kept parallel with the roof of the mouth. The sound expressed by the English word *err** is a Flat vowel.

§57. (2) **The distance between the part of the tongue which articulates and the roof of the mouth.** The exact nature of each vowel, whether made at the back of the mouth or in the front, depends upon the distance between the part of the tongue articulating and the roof of the mouth. By opening the mouth very slowly, so that this distance very gradually increases, we get an almost unlimited number of vowels. From among these we select three more or less arbitrarily, to serve as points of departure. These are called **High, Mid** and **Low.** In a High vowel the passage between the tongue and the roof of the mouth is narrow, just sufficiently large to allow the voice to escape without audible friction. In a Low vowel the tongue is lowered as far as possible from the roof, so that we have the widest possible passage. The Mid vowel stands halfway between these two. Examples: The vowel in *see* is a High vowel; the vowel in *say* is Mid; the vowel in *said* is Low.†

§58. (3) **The condition of the muscles of the tongue.** The nature of vowels is further considerably affected by the condition of the tongue muscles in the part articulating. If these muscles are braced up we have a **Tense** vowel. If they are loose and slack we have a **Slack** vowel.

---

* Scottish students find this sound difficult. By putting a pencil into the mouth the tongue may be kept flat along the bottom of the mouth, and the sound uttered. There is of course no **r** in this word in English.

† This is true of Scottish, but not of English. See chapter on English vowels.

Apart from the differing sensation there is also an audible difference. A Tense vowel has a clear sound, a Slack vowel has a dull sound. The *i* of *marine* is a tense sound, that heard in *pit* is slack.

§ 59. (4) **The movements of the lips.** In many vowels the nature of the sound is also modified by the pursing up or pushing forward of the lips. Such are said to be **Rounded,** The degree of rounding varies normally with the height of the vowel. High vowels have the most rounding, low vowels the least; mid vowels have medium rounding. When the lips retain or assume their ordinary neutral position the vowel is said to be **Unrounded.** The **a** in *man* is unrounded, the **o** in *no* is rounded.

§ 60. **The vowel table.** The following vowel table embodies the four points just discussed.

	TENSE.			SLACK.			
	Back.	Flat.	Front.	Back.	Flat.	Front.	
High, -	1	7	13	19	25	31	Unrounded.
Mid, -	2	8	14	20	26	32	
Low, -	3	9	15	21	27	33	
High, -	4	10	16	22	28	34	Rounded.
Mid, -	5	11	17	23	29	35	
Low, -	6	12	18	24	30	36	

§ 61. Study the table carefully, notice the arrangement and recapitulate the different points.

High, mid, low refer to the up and down movements of
the tongue, hence they are placed vertically on the table.
Back, flat and front represent the horizontal movements, so
they are placed in a straight line.   The lips are supposed to
be at the extreme right, hence the terms referring to them
are placed there—rounded and unrounded; hence also the
back vowels are put on the extreme left, as far as possible
from the lips.   Any vowel may be made tense or slack, so
the table is divided by a central vertical line, to the left of
which are found all the tense vowels, the slack vowels being
on the right.   Rounding of the lips may accompany any
tongue position : above the central horizontal line are the
unrounded vowels, below are the rounded.

In drawing up this table the two central lines, horizontal
and vertical, should always be made more conspicuous than
the other lines.   It is a good plan to use red ink, the rest
of the table being in black.   Number each square; the
vowels are then easily referred to in connexion with the
table.

§ 62. The table contains 36 squares, space accordingly
for 36 vowels.   This does not exhaust all the possibilities.
Each square represents a certain definite position of the
tongue and contains the sound uttered when the tongue is
placed in that position.   For example, square 4 is the home
of the English sound *oo* in *zoo*.   The tongue has back slope,
and the sound is articulated between the back of the tongue
and the soft palate.   Compare now the corresponding
Scottish sound.   The difference in pronunciation is easily
perceptible, yet we do not feel that we have two distinct
vowels.   One is inclined to say : 'Your *oo* is different
from mine.'   The difference is this : in the Scottish *oo* the
tongue, though retaining its back slope, is pushed a little
further forward in the mouth, and the sound is articulated
between the tongue thus advanced, and the back of the

hard palate. Such a vowel is still a back vowel, but it is a new variety and is called an *Outer-Back*.* We must always be ready to consider the possibility of a new vowel being an outer variety of one which we already know.

§ 63. To Outer-Back vowels correspond *Inner-Front* vowels. In these sounds the tongue retains its normal front slope but is at the same time slightly retracted. Thus the short *i*-sound in English, especially when weakly stressed, is inner-front rather than front, as for example, in *pity*.

Each square may contain inner or outer varieties as well as the original normal sound.

Note that advancing a back vowel does not make a flat vowel. A vowel continues to be back so long as it has back tongue slope whether it be retracted or advanced.

§ 64. Two vowels uttered in the same breath impulse form a **Diphthong**. The position of the first element in a diphthong is always difficult to decide, because the tongue does not rest upon it but passes immediately in the direction of the second element.

* Compare Sweet, *Primer of Phonetics*[3], § 37 ; and Sweet, *Sounds of English*, §§ 98-104.

IX.

VOWELS AND DIPHTHONGS OF SCOTTISH.

§ 65. **A. Vowels.** Take the words: *me, may, err.* Say the first aloud, naturally at first, then very slowly, separating as much as possible consonant and vowel, and lastly, isolate the vowel and repeat it several times by itself. Go back then to the original word to make sure that the isolated vowel is precisely the same as the vowel in the word. Now consider how this sound is made. The front of the tongue (cp. § 55) is raised high in the mouth (§ 57) in the direction of the hard palate, the muscles are braced up (§ 58) and the lips are neutral (§ 59). The vowel is accordingly high-front-tense-unrounded. The symbol is i (cp. French *ici*, etc.). Repeat *may* in similar fashion until the vowel can be isolated easily and distinctly; for this the symbol is e (cp. French *été*). For e the distance between the tongue and the roof of the mouth has been widened: it is the mid-front-tense-unrounded vowel.

Now say i, e, and notice the distance the tongue falls, and remember that you are passing from high to mid position.

It is somewhat more difficult to isolate clearly the vowel of *err*. It is best to say the whole word very slowly, separating the vowel from the consonant as much as possible, until the ears become accustomed to the sound of the vowel alone. This sound is articulated like the others,

except that it is the low vowel of the series. Its symbol
is ɛ.

§ 66. Compare the vowel e in *may, made*, etc., with the
vowel in *mud* and *but*. Isolate this latter sound (symbol ɒ)
and compare it again with e. How do they agree? Both
are made with lips neutral, with tightened tongue muscles,
and with a fairly wide distance between the tongue and the
roof of the mouth; both are unrounded, tense and mid.
They differ as regards the place where the sound is articulated. ɒ is made between the back of the tongue and
the soft palate, and is therefore a back vowel.

Repeat frequently ɒ, e and notice the forward movement
of the tongue.

§ 67. Now compare the vowel in *but* with that in *boat*, ɒ
with o. Repeat them and try to discover the difference by
watching your mouth in a mirror. A difference in the
position of the lips is noticed at once. o has the same
tongue position as ɒ, but for it the lips are pushed forward
and rounded. It is mid-back-tense-rounded and belongs
to square 5.

§ 68. Return to the vowel in *me* and compare it with the
vowel in *hit* (symbol *i*). Take a hand-glass and say i, *i*,
raising the head and watching the tongue. Both are high,
front and unrounded, but they differ in the condition of
the tongue's muscles: in i these are tense, but in *i* they
are relaxed or slack. *i* is high-front-slack-unrounded
(square 31).

§ 69. See now if you can discover a vowel standing to o in
the same relation as *i* does to i. Say i–*i*, o–(?), and try to
decide which of your sounds will fill the space. The sound
needed is the *o* of *not, got*, etc., for which the symbol is *o*.
It is mid-back-slack-rounded and fills square 23.

§ 70. Turn to § 62 and read again carefully the description
of outer-back vowels. Say aloud the following words: *put,*

bush, pool, boot.   Isolate the vowel, which for the present may be written **u**.   With the help of a mirror we see that the lips are protruded; it is therefore a rounded vowel. What are the position and condition of the tongue?   If you say χ as in *loch* and then **u**, you will find that the tongue position does not change very greatly; the lips move, of course, and this gives at first a sensation of decided change, but concentrate attention on the back of the tongue and you will find the movement there to be slight.   The vowel then must be made with the back of the tongue, and in the high position, since it is not far from the consonantal position of χ.   It is high-back-rounded.

Is it tense or slack?   This point must be decided by each reader for himself.   I have heard both.   When the sound is uttered with emphasis it is, I think, always tense, but in rapid speech in the West of Scotland the slack sound is not infrequent.

Whether slack or tense it is rarely full-back but almost always outer-back.   A small [2] after the letter shows that it is outer.   The tense vowel is written u^2, the slack u^2 (squares 4 and 22).

§71.   Pronounce aloud the following words : *path, father, hard, hat.*   The first thing to discover is the number of vowel sounds which, in your own pronunciation, these words represent.   Do you divide these words into two groups, or have they all the same sound?   Some Scottish speakers use the same sound in all these words, some pronounce the α in *hard* differently to the other three, others *hard* and *father* alike, and *path* and *hat.*

If *hard* (*father*) are pronounced differently from the others they contain a deeper sound, made somewhat further back in the mouth.   Those who pronounce all the sounds alike may disregard for the moment what is said about the deeper variety, and notice only the description of the other sound.

Say several times i–*i*, and then try to find a vowel which bears the same resemblance to ɒ (in *but*) as *i* does to i.

Say o–ɒ, or, in other words, unround o by keeping the tongue firmly in position and moving the lips back.   Now unround *o*.

The sound which results from both experiments, if correctly performed, is the same, namely, the rather deep ɑ sometimes heard in Scottish *hard*, always in Standard English *father*: the mid-back-slack-unrounded vowel.   The more typical Scottish sound is a slightly advanced variety * of ɑ.   Say again *path*, *pat*, *man*.   The tongue is lowered as well as advanced, and the sound is low-back-outer-unrounded-slack; the symbol is a.

The use of ɑ for all the words under discussion is sometimes heard, but should be avoided.

§ 72. *Butter, author, colour.*   In these three words it is the vowel of the second syllable that we are to discuss. Notice that in all three the sound of the second syllable is the same, though the spelling is different.   The tongue's muscles are relaxed, and the lips are unrounded; so much is easily felt and seen.   We have yet to discover the part of the tongue used, and its distance from the roof of the mouth.   Comparison with i will show that this is not a front vowel, and with u that it is not a back vowel.   The tongue slopes neither to the back nor to the front.   It is therefore a flat vowel.   The tongue is not very close to the roof nor touching the floor of the mouth, so it is a mid vowel.   The symbol is ə and it belongs to square 26.

---

*To reach this sound lower the tongue from ɑ (sq. 20) to another deeper ɑ (sq. 21, normal position), then advance to the outer sound.

§73. Table of Scottish vowels.

	TENSE.			SLACK.			
	Back.	Flat.	Front.	Back.	Flat.	Front.	
High, -	1	7	13 i	19	25	31 *i*	Unrounded.
Mid, -	2 ɒ	8	14 e	20 ɑ	26 ə	32	Unrounded.
Low, -	3	9	15 ɛ	21 a	27	33	Unrounded.
High, -	4 u²	10	16	22 *u²*	28	34	Rounded.
Mid, -	5 o	11	17	23 *o*	29	35	Rounded.
Low, -	6	12	18	24	30	36	Rounded.

§74. **B. Diphthongs.** Take the following words : *chide, tide, tied, apply, fly, pride, pried (pry), child, night, file.* Decide first of all upon the number of diphthongs represented : are there one or two?   There are two at least, in the pronunciation of most Scottish speakers, considered individually, and when a group of speakers is examined, four different types of diphthong may be distinguished.   Say any of these words very slowly, then isolate the diphthong, and lastly try to separate it into its two elements.   It will not be difficult to discover that it consists of some kind of ɑ-sound, followed by some kind of i or *i.*

We will now describe the various types, and it must be the reader's task to assign to his own sounds their proper analysis. (The task is a very difficult one, and beginners

had better be content at first with the general analysis.)
The words *tied* and *tide* may be taken as examples of the
two types of diphthong In *tied* the first and second
elements are slack, a*i*; in *tide* both elements are tense, ɒi.
Another diphthong sometimes takes the place of a*i*, particularly in the pronunciation of men.   In it the first element
is decidedly deeper, probably low-back-slack-unrounded,
and it may be symbolised by ᴀ*i*.   The fourth variety is
more frequently heard from women, and is then commonly
used for all words of this class ; in it a takes the place of ɑ,
and by some the **a** is advanced almost to the low-front
position.   The symbol for this diphthong is a*i*

§ 75. Isolate and try to analyse the diphthong of *house*,
now, etc.   It will be found to consist of some form of ɑ
followed by an u-sound.   Here again different varieties
are heard, and the reader must try to decide upon his own.
The second element is always the high-back-rounded-
advanced vowel, but by some speakers it is pronounced
slack, by others tense.   The first element is either ɑ or ɒ,
the former being more frequently heard now.   The symbols
are au^2 and ɒu^2.

§ 76. The diphthong heard in *coil*, *toy*, etc., consists of
the mid-back-rounded-slack vowel *o*, followed by the high-
front-slack-unrounded *i*, symbol *oi*.

X.

COMPARISON OF SCOTTISH AND STANDARD ENGLISH.

§ 77. The sounds of Scottish differ materially from those of standard English, both as regards vowels and consonants. If a Scottish speaker wishes to speak standard English correctly he must have, first of all, a definite conception of existing differences. He should understand clearly how each sound which he normally pronounces is made, and how it differs from the corresponding sound of the new dialect he is about to acquire. Secondly, he must know how the new sounds he learns are to be distributed; in other words, in what words to use them, and how the distribution of sounds in the new dialect compares with that of the old (cp. Wyld, *The Growth of English*, p. 53; *The Teaching of Reading*, chap. v.). Both tasks are difficult, and require perseverance and patient study. The aim of the present chapter is to indicate the main differences between the form of Scottish we are considering and the standard dialect. As before, the consonants will be dealt with first.

A. Consonants.

§ 78. *The use of* **r**. The most obvious difference in the pronunciation of consonants is the use of *r* by Scottish speakers in positions where English no longer has this sound.   The rules for the pronunciation and omission of *r* in English are:

(1) **r** is pronounced before a vowel-sound (*a*) initial—*rat*, (*b*) medial—*bread, airy*.

(2) **r** is not pronounced (*a*) before a consonant—*art, arm*, (*b*) before a silent vowel—*aired, wares*.

(3) **r** final in a word is silent unless followed immediately by a vowel in a following word—*ba*(*r*), but *bar of iron*.   Even in the latter case some English speakers omit the *r*, but this is not to be imitated.

§ 79. 1.   In forming l in English the tip of the tongue is raised to the teeth-ridge, and the part immediately behind the tip is somewhat hollowed.   This hollowing makes the English l much darker than, for instance, the French l where the part behind the tip is arched.   In Scottish the hollowing is much more considerable than in English, and the l still 'darker.'   Among less educated speakers this is exaggerated to the extent of totally altering the preceding vowel, such pronunciations as *hull* for *hill* resulting.   It is certainly worth while to try and attain the clearer l-sound as being more distinct.   Practice making the tongue convex behind the point, and then only allow it to be very slightly concave.

§ 80. **t, d.**   I have already mentioned (§ 45) the tendency of some Scottish speakers to make these sounds as point-teeth rather than as point consonants before **r**, the result to English ears being that a **th**-sound is heard between the **t** and **r** in *trade*, for example.   This only occurs, as far as I know, when a speaker distinctly trills the **r**, and the two points are, in my opinion, intimately connected.   The pronunciation has a somewhat slovenly effect and is to be avoided.

§ 81. ç and χ (cp. §§ 47, 48).   These sounds are not

heard in standard English, and most English speakers find them difficult to acquire, and substitute **k**.

§ 82. **w, ᴍ**. Scottish speakers preserve the distinction between these two sounds, pronouncing ᴍ wherever the spelling has *wh*. In standard English, especially in the South, the voiceless sound does not occur, *witch* and *which* being alike pronounced **wɪtʃ**.

§ 83. ð, þ. The formation of these two consonants is identical in English and Scottish, but the distribution is somewhat different. The voiceless sound occurs more frequently in Scottish than in English. The following is a list of those words which in standard English have a voiced initial : *than, that, the, thee, thou, thy, thine, their, them, then, thence, there, these, they, this, thither, those, though, thus.* Scottish readers should mark any word in this list in which they vary from the standard sound : *thither, thence,* and *though* have usually a voiceless initial in Scottish.

Further, the standard dialect has *wɪð, wɪðaut*, whereas in both these words þ is commonly used in Scottish.

B. Vowels.

§ 84. *i* in *bit, little, pretty,* etc. In English the tendency, especially in unstressed syllables, is to retract this vowel. In Scottish the vowel is often lowered towards the mid-position. Highland speakers pronounce a high vowel, but make it tense. Great care should be taken to keep the tongue in the high-front-slack position (§§ 56-58), and to make a clear *i*-sound.

§ 85. i in *heed, me, marine,* etc. This vowel is high-front-tense-unrounded. In English it is long or diphthongised (cp. § 96(*a*)). Scottish speakers pronounce it half-long.

§ 86. *e* in *bet, red, den.* This vowel is mid-front-slack, and is very characteristic of English. Scottish speakers substitute ɛ, that is, they lower the tongue and tighten its muscles. In the opinion of some phoneticians the Scottish ε only varies from the English in being lowered, coming thus near the æ-position, but I am unable to agree with this view.

In Scottish this vowel is usually pronounced half-long.

§ 87. æ in *man, bad, shall*, the low-front-slack vowel. The most frequent sound heard in Scottish in these words is a (cp. § 71), but ɑ is also possible. I have heard ɑ more frequently from men than from women.

§ 88. ε. Low-front-tense. In English this sound never occurs alone, but always in close combination with the sound ə, the two together forming a diphthong. 'Examples: *air*, εə; *share*, ʃεə. Notice that in these words Scottish has quite a different vowel, namely, e, and that the r is pronounced—English, εə, Scottish, er.

§ 89. ɑ in *father, heart, path*, the mid-back-slack-unrounded vowel. Some Scottish speakers use this vowel in these words, while others substitute a (cp. § 71).

§ 90. ʊ in *run, come*. In English generally pronounced as the mid-back-slack-outer; in Scottish this sound is sometimes heard, but the mid-back-tense is more general.

§ 91. u in *mood, rude*, and u in *full, good*. The former of these two sounds is, in English, sometimes a diphthong (cp. § 96(*c*)), if not, it is the rounded-high-back-tense vowel pronounced long. The latter sound is high-back rounded-slack and short. In Scottish no distinction is made between these two classes of u-sound. For both Scottish speakers substitute an outer high-back-rounded vowel (cp. § 62). The quantity is also different from either of the English vowels, it is shorter than the long u of *mood* but longer than the u of *full*.

In weakly-stressed syllables this sound occurs short.

§ 92. ɔ in *law*, ɒ in *not, got*. These sounds differ precisely as did the preceding; both sounds are low-rounded-back, but the former is tense and long and the latter slack and short. Scottish substitutes for both the mid-back-rounded-slack half-long or short (§ 69).

Note that the English ɔ in *law* is distinctly over-rounded.

§ 93. ʌ as in *err, bird, churn*. These words have all the same vowel-sound in English, the *r* being of course silent. It is the low-flat-unrounded-tense vowel. It is not a sound which occurs in Scottish, but can be learned without diffi-culty. The tongue must be kept flat along the bottom of the mouth, and in first attempts it is useful to put a pencil in one's mouth to preserve the low-flat position of the tongue. A Scotchman pronouncing in his natural speech the three words given above will note that the English ʌ-sound takes the place of several different Scottish vowels.

§ 94. ə. The latter vowel in *butter, rather*, is mid-flat-slack-unrounded. This vowel occurs in English only in unstressed syllables. It is of very frequent occurrence, since it takes the place of other vowels when these become unstressed through their position in the sentence. Thus, compare the differences in the word *was* in the following sentences: ' I tell you it was,' ' They said he was coming now.'

In Scottish this ə has a different distribution. It is used sometimes where English would use *i*, for example, **fesəz, wimən**, etc. On the other hand, it is often not used in Scottish where it would be used in English. In its place occur weakened varieties of the original vowel, or in the case of some speakers, the mid-flat-tense-unrounded sound.

The Diphthongs.

§ 95. One of the characteristics of standard English is a strong tendency to diphthongise long vowel-sounds. This tendency is not shared by Scottish speakers.

The English diphthongs with their Scotch equivalents may be divided into three classes.

§ 96. 1. *So-called 'long' English vowels which are in reality diphthongs.*

(*a*) The sound in *heed, meat,* etc. (cp. § 85). The first element in this diphthong is the high-front-tense-unrounded vowel i. The speaker begins to pronounce with his tongue in position for this high-front vowel but fails to keep the tongue steady. He raises it slightly before the sound is finished, and by so doing passes from the high vowel position to the adjacent middle-open consonant position j. The symbol for this diphthong is ij. Note that the consonantal element is very slight and by many speakers omitted entirely. The corresponding vowel in Scottish is the high-front-tense unrounded without any trace of diphthongisation.

(*b*) The sound in *may, change, take.* This sound is invariably diphthongised by all speakers of standard English. Its first element is the mid-front-slack-unrounded vowel, its second the high-front-slack-unrounded. The symbol is *ei.* Note that this diphthong and the foregoing illustrate the tendency in English to lift the tip of the tongue. It is very difficult for an English speaker to keep the tongue still throughout the whole of a long sound. Hence their many difficulties with the pronunciation of French for example.

(*c*) The sound in *mood, rude,* etc. The first element is the high-back-tense-rounded vowel, and diphthongisation is heard when lips and tongue are not kept perfectly steady throughout the enunciation of the sound. By a slight extra rounding of the lips w is reached. The symbol for the diphthong is uw. As in the case of the previous sound diphthongisation is not invariable even among speakers of standard English (cp. § 91), and it is absent in Scottish.

(*d*) The sound in *no, told, shoulder,* etc. The first sound is the mid-back-tense-rounded vowel, but before the sound

is finished the lips have moved forward a little, producing
the effect of a high-back-rounded vowel.   Possibly the
tongue moves upwards too.   The symbol is **ou**.   Note that
where there is no rounding of the original vowel, diphthongisation is caused by a slight upward movement of the
tip of the tongue, **ij**, *ei*; where there is rounding the forward
movement of the lips is responsible for the introduction of
a second element, **ou, uw**.

§97.   2. *The murmur diphthongs of English.*

A number of diphthongs arise in English through the loss
of **r** in pronunciation, though not in spelling, and the sub-
stitution of **ə** (cp. §78), which, with the preceding vowel,
forms a diphthong.   In Scottish the **r** is pronounced, so
such diphthongs do not arise.

(*a*) *ear, cheer, mere,* etc.   English *i*ə, Scottish **ir**; English
tʃ*i*ə, Scottish **tʃir**; English m*i*ə, Scottish **mir**.

(*b*) *pair, share,* etc.   English p**ɛ**ə, Scottish **per**; English
ʃɛə, Scottish **ʃer**.

(*c*) *poor, cure, skewer,* etc.   English **puə**,* Scottish **pu²r**;
English **kjuə**, Scottish **kjur**; English **skjuə**, Scottish **skju²r**.

(*d*) *shore, oar, door,* etc.   English ʃɔə,† Scottish **ʃor**;
English ɔə, Scottish **ɔr**; English dɔə, Scottish **dor**.

§98.   3. *Diphthongs occurring in English and Scottish.*

(*a*) The sound in *high, fly, file,* etc.   The comparison of
English and Scottish is complicated by the different varieties
of this diphthong at present heard in Scottish (cp. §74).
In English the diphthong consists of the advanced **a** sound

---

* Several other pronunciations are possible (cp, Wyld, *Growth of
English*, p. 36).

† By many speakers the **ə** is dropped in these words, the sound in
their case ceasing to be a diphthong.

(cp. §71), followed by a retracted *i* (symbol a*i*). In Scotland the original native sound would appear to be ɒi (cp.
§74), which is being abandoned more or less consciously.
The sounds heard now are ɒi, ɑ*i*, and a*i*. Among those
who pronounce the last there is a tendency to exaggerate
the advancing of a till a diphthong, which we may write æ*i*,
results. This has an affected sound and should be avoided.

(*b*) The sound in *house, town*, etc. The symbol ɑ*u* fairly
represents this diphthong as it is heard in English. It
is mid-back-slack-unrounded followed by high-back-slack-
rounded. The chief difference in Scottish is the substi-
tution of u^2 for the English *u*. Further, ɒ is sometimes
heard for ɑ.

(*c*) The sound in *boy, coil, joy*. The first element in this
diphthong in English is the low-back-tense vowel normally
rounded, lacking, that is, the over-rounding which it receives
when it stands alone.† Scottish speakers substitute the
mid-back-slack-rounded vowel, and there is a tendency to
under-round or lower it. Symbols: English ɔ*i*, Scottish o*i*.†

† For slightly different analyses see Sweet, *Primer of Phonetics*, 3rd ed.
§ 201 ; Jones, *Pronunciation of English*, § 145; Wyld, *Growth of
English*, p. 35.

Texts.

A. Scottish.†

1. roz elmər.—baɪ wɒltər savɪdʒ landər.

   ɑ ʍɒt əvelz ðə sɛptərd res?
   ɑ ʍɒt ðə fɔrm dɪvaɪn?
   ʍɒt ɛvrɪ vərtju² ɛvrɪ gres?
   roz elmər, ɒl wər ðaɪn.

   roz elmər hu²m ðiz wekfu²l ɑɪz
   me wɪp, bɒt nɛvər si;
   ə naɪt əv mɛmərɪz ən saɪz,
   ɑɪ kɒnsɪkret tə ði.

NOTES.

1. One student told me she had always used the diphthong ɒi until at school she was taught to say aɪ.

2. The pronunciation 'virtju²' was given by one speaker.

3. Several students pronounced 'naɪt.'

4. 'Ah!' was pronounced ɑ by some, and **a** by others.

5. For English version of this and the two following texts, cp. Wyld, *Teaching of Reading*, pp. 99, 103, and 78.

2. ðə dɛþbɛd.—tɒməs hu²d.

   wi wɒtʃt hər brɪðɪŋ, þru² ðə nɒit,
   hər brɪðɪŋ sɒft ənd lo,
   əz ɪn hər brɛst ðə wev əv laɪf
   kɛpt hivɪng tu² ən fro.

   so saɪləntlɪ wi simd tu² spik,
   so slolɪ mu²vd əbɑu²t,
   əz wi həd lɛnt hər hɑf ɑu²r pɑu²rz
   tu² ik hər lɪvɪŋ ɑu²t.

† Texts 1, 2, 3, were prepared by groups of students.

aɷ²r vɛrɪ hops bɪlaɪd aɷ²r firz,
aɷ²r firz aɷ²r hops bɪlaɪd—
wi þot hər daɪɪŋ ʍɛn ʃi slɛpt,
and slipɪŋ ʍɛn ʃɪ daɪd.

for ʍɛn ðə morn kem dɪm ənd sad,
ən(d) tʃɪl wɪþ ɛrlɪ ʃaɷ²rz,
hər kwaɪət aɪlɪdz klozd—ʃi had
ənɒðər morn ðən aɷ²rz.

3. ðə twɛlfþ tʃaptər əv ɪklizɪastiz, vɛrsɪz wɒn tə sɛvn.

rɪmɛmbər naɷ² ðaɪ krietər ɪn ðə dez əv ðaɪ juˀþ, ʍaɪl ði
ivl dez kɒm nɒt, nor ðə jɪrz dro naɪ, ʍɛn ðaɷ² ʃlt se aɪ hav
no plɛʒər ɪn ðɛm. ʍaɪl ðə sɒn, or ðə laɪt, or ðə muˀn, or ðə
starz bɪ nɒt darkənd, nor ðə klaɷ²dz rɪtɔrn aftər ðə ren : ɪn ðə
de ʍɛn ðə kipərz əv ðə haɷ²s ʃəl trɛmbl, ənd ðə strɒɪ mɛn
ʃəl baɷ² ðɛmsɛlvɪ, ənd ðə graɪndərz sɪs bɪkoz ðe ar fju², ənd
ðoz ðət luˀk aɷ²t əv ðə wɪndoz bi daɪkənd, ənd ðə dorz ʃl bi
ʃɒt ɪn ðə strɪts, ʍɛn ðə saɷ²nd əv ðə graɪndɪŋ ɪz lo, ənd hi ʃl
raɪɪ ɒp at ðə voɪs əv ðə bɒrd, ənd ɒl ðə dotərz əv mju²zik ʃl bi
brɒt lo ; ɒlso ʍɛn ðe ʃl bi afred əv ðat ʍɪtʃ ɪz haɪ, ənd fɪɪz
ʃl bi ɪn ðə we, ənd ði amənd tri ʃl flɒrɪʃ, ənd ðə grashopər ʃl
bi ə bɒrdən, ənd dɪzaɪr ʃl fel: bɪkoz man goɛþ tuˀ ɪz lɒŋ hom
ənd ðə mornərz go əbaɷ²t ðə strɪts : or ɛvər ði sɪlvər kɒrd bɪ
luˀst, or ðə goldn bol bɪ brokn, or ðə pɪtʃər bɪ brokn ət ðə
faɷ²ntn, or ðə ʍil bɪ brokn ət ðə sɪstərn. ðɛn ʃal ðə dɒst rɪtɔrn
tuˀ ðə ɛrþ əz ɪt woz, ənd ðə spɪrɪt ʃl rɪtɔrn tuˀ god huˀ gev ɪt.

4. frəm karlaɪlz ɛsɪ ɒn bɒrnz.*

ði ɛksələns əv bɒrnz ɪz ɪndɪd əmɒŋ ðə rɛrəst, ʍɛðər ɪn
poɪtrɪ or proz, bt ət ðə sem tɒim ɪt ɪz plen ənd ɪzɪlɪ rɛkəg-
naɪzd : hɪz sɪnsɛrɪtɪ, hɪz ɪndɪspjətəbl er əv truˀþ. hir ər no

* Prepared from the educated speech of the West of Scotland. The
degree of advancing of u varies in different speakers, in some it ıs
hardly advanced at all. e is sometimes heard instead of ɛ in words
which ın standard English have ɛ.

ʃabju²ləs woz ɒr dʒɔiz ; no hɒlo fəntastɪk sɛntɪməntalɪtɪz ;
no wɑɪrdrɒn rɪʃɑɪnɪŋz, ɑɪðər ɪn þɒt ɒr filɪŋ : ðə paʃən ðət ɪz
trest bɪfor ɒs haz glod ɪn ə lɪvɪŋ hɑrt ; ðɪ opɪnjən hi ɒtərz
həz rɪzn ɪn hɪz on ɒndərstandɪŋ, ənd bin ə lɑɪt tu² ɪz on stɛps.
hi dɒz not rɑɪt frəm hirse, bət frəm sɑɪt ənd ɪkspirɪəns, it ɪz
ðə sinz ðt hi əz lɪvd ənd lebərd əmɪdst ðt hi dɪskrɑɪbz ; ðoz
sinz, ru²d ənd hɒmbl əz ðe ɑr, həv kɪndld bju²tɪʃũ²l ɪmoʃənz
ɪn hɪz sol, nobl þɒts, ən dɛfɪnət rɪzɒlvz ; ənd hi spiks fɒrþ
ʍot iz ɪn hɪm, not frəm ɛnɪ ɑu²twərd kɒl əv vanɪtɪ ɒr ɪntərəst,
bt bɪkɒz hɪz hɑrt ɪz tu² fu²l tə bɪ sɑɪlənt. hi spiks ɪt wɪþ
sɒtʃ mɛlɒdɪ ənd mɒdju²leʃn əz hi kan ; in homlɪ rɒstɪk
dʒɪŋgl ; bt ɪt ɪz hɪz on ən dʒɛnju²ɪn. ðɪs ɪz ðə grand sikrət
fŏr ʃɑɪndɪŋ ridərz ənd rɪtenɪŋ ðəm : lɛt hɪm hu² ᴡu²d mu²v
ənd kənvɪns ɒðərz, bi fərst mu²vd ənd kənvɪnst hɪmsɛlf. tu²
ɛvrɪ poɪt, tu ɛvrɪ rɑɪtər, wi mɑɪt se : bi tru², ɪf ju² wu²d bi
bɪlivd. lɛt ə man bt spik fɒrþ wɪþ dʒɛnju²ɪn ərnəstnəs ðə
þɒt, ðɪ ɪmoʃən. ðɪ aktju²əl kəndɪʃən əv hɪz ou hart ; ənd ɒðər
mɛn, so strendʒlɪ ɒr wi ol nɪt təgɛðər bɑɪ ðə tɑɪ əv sɪmpəþɪ,
mɒst ənd wɪl gɪv hid tə hɪm. ɪn kɒltjər, ɪn ɪkstɛnt əv vju²,
wi me stand əbɒv ðə spikər ɒr bɪlo hɪm ; bət ɪn ɑɪðər kes,
hɪz wɒrdz, if ðe ɑr ərnɪst ənd sɪnsir, wɪl fɑɪnd sɒm rɪspɒns
wɪþɪn ‖ ɒs ; fər ɪn spɑɪt əv ol kaʒu²əl vərɑiɪtɪz ɪn ɑu²twərd
raŋk, ŏr ɪnwərd, az fes ansərz tu² fes, so dɒz ðɪ hɑrt əv man
tu² man.

5. frɒm ' mɛmorɪz † ənd portrəts.'—bɑɪ ɑr ɛl stivənsən.*

ðə dɪvɪʒən əv resɔz ɪz mor ʃɑrplɪ mɑrkt wɪþɪn ðə bɒrdərz
əv skɒtlənd ɪtsɛlf ðɑn bətwin ðə kɒntrɪz.† gɑlowe ənd
bɒχən, loðɪɑn ənd loχɑbər, ɑr lɒik forɪn pɑrts ; jet ju² me
tʃu²z ə man frɒm ɛnɪ əv ðəm, ənd, tɛn tə wɒn, hi ʃɑl pru²v
tũ² həv ðə hɛd mɑrk əv ə skɒt. ə sɛntju²rɪ ənd ə hɑf əgo ðə

‖ Or wɪðɪn.
† The unstressed *i* is pronounced half-tense.
* Prepared by W. L. Renwick, Glasgow.

hɒiləndər wor ə dɪfərənt kɒstjŭ²m, spok ə dɪfərənt laŋwɪdʒ,
wɒrʃɪpt ɪn ənɒðər tʃɒrtʃ, hɛld dɪfərənt mɒrəlz, ənd obed ə
dɪfərənt soʃəl kɒnstɪtju²ʃn from hɪz fɛlo-kɒntrɪmən ɪðər əv ðə
sɒu²þ or norþ   ivən ðə eŋglɪʃ,‡ ɪt ɪz rəkɒrdəd, dɪd nɒt loþ
ðə hɒiləndər ənd ðə hɒilənd kɒstju²m az ðe wɛr loðd baɪ ðə
rəmendər əv ðə skɒtʃ. jɛt ðə hɒiləndər fɛlt hɪmsɛlf ə skɒt.
hi wu²d wɪlɪŋlɪ red intŭ² ðə skɒtʃ loləndz ; bɒt hɪz kɒrədʒ
feld hɪm ət ðə bɒrdər, ənd hi rəgɑrdəd eŋglənd ‡ əz ə pɛrɪlɒs
ɒnhomlɪ lɑnd.   ʌɛn ðə blɑk wɒtʃ, aftər jɪrz əv fɒrɪn sɛrvɪs
rətɒrnd tŭ² skɒtlənd, vɛtərənz lipt ɒu²t ənd kɪst ði ɛrþ ət port-
pɑtrɪk.   ðe həd bɪn ɪn aɪrlənd, steʃnd əmɒŋ mɛn əv ðər
on res ənd laŋwɪdʒ, ʌer ðe wɛr wɛl lɒikt ənd tritəd wɪþ
afɛkʃn , bɒt ɪt wɒz ðə soɪl əv galɒwe ðət ðe kɪst ət ðə ɛk-trɪm
ɛnd əv ðə hɒstɒil loləndz, əmɒŋ ə pipl hu² dɪd nɒt ɒndər-
stɑnd ðer spitʃ, ənd hu² həd hetəd, hɑrɪd.† ənd haŋd ðəm
sɪns ðə dɒn əv hɪstərɪ.†   lɑst, ənd pərhɑps most kju²rɪəs, ðə
sɒnz əv tʃɪftənz wər ofɒ ɛdju²ketəd ɒn ðə kɒntɪnənt əv ju²rəp.
ðe wɛnt əbrɒd spikɪŋ galɪk, ðe rətɒrnd spikɪŋ nɒt eŋglɪʃ,‡ bɒt
ðə brɒd daɪəlɛkt əv skɒtlənd.   nɒu², ʌɒt aɪdɪə had e ɪn ðer
mɒindz ʌɛn ðe ðɒs, ɪn þɒt, aɪdɛntɪfaɪd ðəmsɛlvz wɪþ ðer
ɑnsɛstrəl ɛnəmiz?† ʌɒt wəz ðə sɛns ɪn ʌɪtʃ ðe wər skɒtʃ ənd
nɒt eŋglɪʃ, or skɒtʃ ənd nɒt aɪrɪʃ? kɑn ə ber nem bi ðɒs
ɪnflu²ɛnʃl ɒn ðə mɒindz ənd ɒfɛkʃnz əv mɛn, ənd ə polɪtɪkəl
agrɛgeʃn blɒind ðəm tŭ² ðə netjŭ²r əv fɑkts ?

ðə storɪ əv ðə ɒstrɪən ɛmpaɪr wu²d sɪm tŭ² ɑnsər, no ; ðə
fɑr mor golɪŋ bɪznəs əv aɪrlənd klɛnʃəz ðə nɛgatɪv from nirər
hom.   ɪz ɪt kɒmən ɛdju²keʃn, kɒmən mɒrəlz, ə kɒmən
laŋwɪdʒ or ə kɒmən feþ, ðət dʒɒɪn mɛn ɪntŭ² neʃnz? ðer
wɛr prɑktɪkəlɪ nɒn əv ðɪz ɪn ðə kes wi ɑr kɒnsɪdərɪŋ.

ðə fɑkt rəmenz : ɪn spɒit əv ðə dɪfərəns əv blɒd ənd
laŋgwɪdʒ, ðə loləndər fɪlz hɪmsɛlf ðə sɛntɪmɛntəl kɒntrɪmən
əv ðə hɒiləndər. ʌɛn ðe mɪt əbrɒd, ðe fol əpon ɪtʃ ɒðərz

<hr>

† The unstressed *i* is pronounced half-tense.
‡ Between *e* and *i*.

nɛks *i*n sp*i*r*i*t ; ivn ət hom ðer *i*z ə kʋind əv klɑn*i*ʃ *i*nt*i*məs*i* *i*n ðər tʋk.

.   .   .   .   .   .

nʋr mʋst wi om*i*t ðə sɛns əv ðə netju²r əv h*i*z kʋntr*i* ənd h*i*z kʋntr*i*z† h*i*stor*i*† grɑdju²əl*i* gro*i*ŋ *i*n ðə tʃʋildz mʋind from stor*i* ənd from *o*bzərveʃn.   ə skot*i*ʃ tʃʋild hirz mʋtʃ əv ʃ*i*prɛk, ʋu²tlɑ*ii*ŋ ɑ*i*rən skɛr*i*z,† p*i*t*i*ləs brekərz, ənd gret si-lʋits ; mʋtʃ əv heðər*i* mʋu²ntənz, wʋild klɑnz, ənd hʋntəd kʋvənɑntərz. brɛþs kʋm tu² h*i*m *i*n soŋ əv ðə d*i*stənt tʃiv*i*ots ənd ðə r*i*ŋ əv fore*i*ŋ hu²fs.   hi glor*i*z† *i*n h*i*z hɑrdf*i*stəd forfɑðərz, əv ðə ɑ*i*rən gərdl ənd ðə hɑndfü²l əv mil, hu² rod so sw*i*ftl*i* ənd l*i*vd so sperl*i* *o*n ðer redz.   pʋvərt*i*, *i*l-lʋk, ɛntərprɑ*i*z, ənd kʋnstənt rɛzʋlju²ʃn ɑr ðə fɑ*i*brz əv ðə lɛdʒənd əv h*i*z kʋntriz h*i*stor*i*.†   ðə hiroz ənd kiŋz əv skʋtlənd hɑv bin trɑdʒ*i*kəl*i* fetəd ; ðə most mɑrkiŋ *i*ns*i*dənts *i*n skot*i*ʃ h*i*stor*i*—flʋdən, der*i*ən, *o*r ðə fʋrt*i*-fɑ*i*v—wər st*i*l *i*ðər felju²rz *o*r dəfitz ; ənd ðə fʋl əv wʋləs ənd ðə rəpitəd rəvɛrsəz əv ðə bru²s cʋmbʋin w*i*þ ðə vɛr*i*† smʋlnəs əv ðə kʋntr*i* tə titʃ rɑðər ə morəl ðən ə mɑtir*i*əl krɑ*i*tir*i*on fʋr lʋif.

6. ði old iŋgl*i*ʃ plez.*—frəm mək*o*l*i*z ɛs*i* *o*n drɑ*i*dən.

nʋ spiʃəz əv f*i*kʃn *i*z so dəlʋitfəl tu² əs əz ði old *i*ŋgl*i*ʃ drama.   ivn *i*ts *i*nfir*i*ər prədʋkʃnz pʋzɛs ə tʃɑrm n*o*t tə bə fɑu²nd *i*n ɛn*i* ʋðər kʋind əv po*i*tr*i*.   *i*t *i*z ðə most lu²s*i*d m*i*rər ðət *i*vər wəz held ʋp tə netʃər.   ðə krieʃnz əv · ðə gret drɑmət*i*sts əv aþənz prədʒu²s ði əfɛkt əv magn*i*fəsənt skʋlptʃərz, kənsivd bɑ*i* ə mʋit*i* *i*madʒəneʃn, pʋl*i*ʃt w*i*þ þi ʋtməst del*i*kəs*i*, əmb*o*d*ii*ŋ ɑidiəz əv *i*nɛfəbl madʒəst*i* ənd bju²t*i*, bət kold, pel, ənd r*i*dʒ*i*d, w*i*þ no blu²m ʋn ðə tʃik, ənd no spɛkjəleʃn *i*n ði ɑ*i*.   *i*n *o*l ðə drepərəz, ðə f*i*gjərz, ənd ðə fesəz, *i*n ðə lʋvərz ənd ðə tɑ*i*rənts, ðə bakənəlz ənd ðə

---

† The unstressed *i* is pronounced half-tense.

* Prepared by T. R. Allison, Paisley.

fju²rəz, ðər əz ðə sem marbl tʃɪlnəs ənd dɛdnəs.   most əv ðə
karəktərz əv ðə frɛnʃ stedʒ rəzɛmbl ðə waksən dʒɛntlmən
ənd ledəz ɪn ðə wɪndo əv ə pərfju²mər, ru²ʒd, kɒrld, ənd
bədɪzənd, bət fɪkst ɪn sɒtʃ stɪf atɪtʃu²dz, ənd sterɪŋ wɪþ aɪz
əksprɛsəv əv sɒtʃ ɒtər ɒnminɪŋnəs, ðət ðe kanət prədʒu²s ən
ɪlu²ʒ(ə)n fər ə sɪŋgl momənt.   ɪn ði ɪŋglɪʃ plez əlon ɪz tə bə
faʊ²nd ðə wormþ, ðə mɛlonəs, ənd ðə rialɪtɪ əv pentɪŋ.   wi
no ðə mɒindz əv ðə mɛn ənd wɪmən, əz wi no ðə fesəz əv ðə
mɛn ənd wɪmən əv vandɒik.

7. Psalm c.*

ɔl pipl ðət ən ɛrþ du dwɛl,
sɪŋ tŭ ðə lord wɪþ tʃirfŭl voɪs,
hɪm sɛrv wɪþ mərþ, hɪz prez forþtɛl
kɒm ji bɪfor hɪm ənd rɪdʒoɪs.

no ðət ðə lord ɪz gɒd ɪndɪd,
wɪþaʊt aʊr ed hi dɪd ɒs mek,
wi ar hɪz flɒk, hi dɒþ ɒs fid
and fər hɪz ʃip hi dɒþ ɒs tek.

o ɛntər ðɛn hɪz gets wɪþ prez,
əprotʃ wɪþ dʒoɪ hɪz korts ɒntu,
prez lɒd ənd blɛs hɪs nem ɔlwez
fər ɪt ɪz simlɪ so tŭ du.

fər ʍaɪ ðə lord aʊr gɒd ɪz gud
hɪz mɛrsɪ ɪz fər ɛvər ʃur
hɪz truþ ət ɔl taɪmz fərmlɪ stud
and ʃal frəm edʒ tu edʒ ɪndjur,

---

* This and the following are prepared by Mr. Grant, Lecturer on
Phonetics in Aberdeen, and represent the educated speech of that
district. The u-sounds are only advanced very slightly if at all.

8. Shakespeare.

ɒðərz əbaɪd aʋr kwɛstjən, ðau ərt fri
wi ɑsk ənd ɑsk. ðaʋ smaɪləst ənd ərt stɪl,
aʋtopɪŋ nɒlɪdʒ. fɒr ðə lɒftɪəst hɪl
hu tŭ ðə stɑrz ɒnkraʋnz hɪz madʒəstɪ
plantɪŋ hɪz stɛdfɑst fŭtstɛps ɪn ðə si,
mekɪŋ ðə hɛvn əv hɛvnz hɪz dwɛlɪŋ-ples,
sperz bət ðə klaʋdɪ bɒrdər əv hɪz bes
tŭ ðə fɔɪld sɛrtʃɪŋ əv mɒrtalɪtɪ,
ən ðaʋ hu dɪdst ðə stɑrz ənd sʋnbimz no,
sɛlf skuld, sɛlf-skand, sɛlf ɒnərd, sɛlf sɪkjur.
dɪdst trɛd ən ɛrþ ɒngɛst at—bɛtər so.
ɔl penz ði ɪmɒrtəl spɪrɪt mʋst ɪndjur,
ɔl wiknəs ʍɪtʃ ɪmperz, ɔl grifs ʍɪtʃ baʋ
faɪnd ðər sol spitʃ ɪn ðat vɪktorɪəs braʋ.

maþju ɑrnəld.

B. English.

9. ə sɒnət.—baɪ sæmjuəl dænjəl.

kɛə-tʃɑːmə sliːp! sɒn əv ðə seɪbl naɪt!
bɹɒðə tə deþ! ɪn saɪlənt dɑːknəs, bɔɪn!
ɹɪliːv maɪ æŋgwiʃ, ənd ɹɪstɔ ðə laɪt!
wɪð dɑːk fəgetɪŋ əv maɪ kɛɒz, ɹɪtʌɪn!
ənd let ðə deɪ bɪ taɪm ɪnɒf tə mɔːn
ðə ʃɪþɹɛk əv maɪ ɪlədventʃəd juːþ!
let weɪkɪŋ aɪz səfaɪs tə weɪl ðɛə skɔɪn,
wɪðaʋt ðə tɔɪment əv ðə naɪts ɒntɹuːþ!
siːs, dɹiːmz! ði ɪmədʒɹɪ əv ɑː deɪ-dɪzaɪəz
tə mɒdl fɔɪþ ðə pæʃənz əv ðə mɒɹou!

nevə let ɹaizɪŋ sɒn əpɹuɪv ju laɪəz!
tu æd mɔɪ gɹiɪf tu ægɹiveɪt maɪ sɔɹou.
stɪl let mi sliɪp! ɪmbɹeɪsɪŋ klaudz in vein;
ən(d) nevə weɪk tə fiɪl ðə deɪz dɪsdein.

10. oud tə djuɪtɪ.—baɪ wɪljəm wʌɹdzwəþ.

stʌɪn dɔɪtəɹ əv də vɔɪs əv gɒd!
ou djuɪtɪ! ɪf ðæt neɪm ðau lɒv
huɪ aɪt ə laɪt tə gaɪd, ə ɹɒd
tə tʃek ði ʌɹɹɪŋ ənd ɹɪpɹuɪv;
ðau huɪ aɪt vɪktəɹɪ ənd lɔɪ
ʍen emtɪ teɹəz ouvəɹɔɪ;
fɹəm vein tempteɪʃənz dɒst set fɹiɪ;
ənd kaɪmst ðə wɪəɹɪ stɹaɪf əv fɹeɪl hjuɪmænɪtɪ!

ðɛəɹ aɪ huɪ aɪsk nɒt ɪf ðaɪn aɪ
bɪ ɒn ðəm; huɪ, in lɒv ənd tɹuɪþ,
ʍɛə nou mɪsgɪvɪŋ ɪz, ɹɪlaɪ
əpɒn ðə dʒiɪnjəl sens əv juɪþ:
glæd haɪts! wɪðaut ɹɪpɹoutʃ ɔɪ blɒt;
huɪ duɪ ðaɪ wʌɪk, ənd nou ɪt nɒt:
ou! ɪf þɹuɪ kɒnfɪdəns mɪspleɪst
ðeɪ feɪl, ðaɪ seɪvɪŋ aɪmz, dɹɛd pɒuə! əɹaund ðəm kaɪst.

.   .   .   .

stʌɪn lɔɪgɪvə. jet ðau dɒst wɛə
ðə gɒdhedz moust bɪnɪgnənt gɹeɪs;
nɔɪ nou wiɪ enɪþɪŋ sou fɛə
æz ɪz ðə smaɪl əpɒn ðaɪ feɪs;
flauəz laɪf bɪfɔɪ ðiɪ ɒn ðɛə bedz,
ənd fɹeɪgɹəns in ðaɪ futɪŋ tɹedz;
ðau dɒst pɹɪsʌɪv ðə staɪz fɹəm ɹɒŋ;
ənd ðə moust eɪnʃənt hevənz, þɹuɪ ðiɪ, aɪ fɹeʃ ənd stɹɒŋ.

11. oud tu ɔɪtəm.—baɪ dʒɔn kiɪts.

siɪzn əv mɪsts ənd melou fɹuɪtfʊlnəs,
klous buzm-fɹend əv ðə mətjuɹɪŋ sʊn;
kənspaɹɪŋ wɪð hɪm hau tə loud ənd blɛs
wɪð fɹuɪt ðə vaɪnz ðət ɹaund ðə þætʃ-iɪvz ɹʊn;
tə bend wɪð æpəlz ðə mɔst kɔtɪdʒ-tɹiɪz
ənd fɪl ɔɪl fɹuɪt wɪð ɹaɪpnəs tu ðə kɔɪ;
tə swɛl ðə guɪəd, ənd plɒmp ðə heɪzl ʃɛlz
wɪð ə swiɪt kʌɪnəl; tə sɛt bɒdɪŋ mɔɪ,
ənd stɪl mɔɪ, leɪtə flauəz fɔ ðə biɪz
ɒntɪl ðeɪ þɪŋk wɔɪm deɪz wɪl nevə siɪs,
fɔ sʊmə hæz ɔɪ-bɹɪmd ðɛə klæmɪ sɛlz.

huɪ hæþ nɔt siɪn ðiɪ ɔft əmɪd ðaɪ stɔɪ?
sʊmtaɪmz huevə siɪks əbɹɔɪd meɪ faɪnd
ðiɪ sɪtɪŋ keələs ɔn ə gɹænəɹɪ flɔɪ,
ðaɪ hɛə sɔft-lɪftɪd baɪ ðə wɪnouɪŋ waɪnd;
ɔɪ ɔn ə hɑɪf-ɹiɪpt fʊɹou saund əsliɪp,
dɹauzd wɪð ðə ʃjuɪm əv pɔpɪz, ʍaɪl ðaɪ huk
spɛəz ðə nɛkst swɔɪþ ənd ɔɪl ɪts twaɪnɪd flauəz:
ənd sʊmtaɪmz laɪk ə gliɪnə ðau dɒst kiɪp
stedɪ ðaɪ leɪdən hed əkɹʋs ə bɹuk;
ɔɪ baɪ ə saɪdə-pɹɛs, wɪð peɪʃənt lʊk
ðau wɔtʃəst ðə laɪst uɪzɪŋz, auəz baɪ auəz.

ʍɛɹ aɪ ðə sɔŋz əv spɹɪŋ? aɪ, ʍɛɹ aɪ ðeɪ?
þɪŋk nɔt əv ðem, ðau hæst ðaɪ mjuɪzɪk tuɪ,—
ʍaɪl bɑɹɹɪd klaudz bluɪm ðə sɔft daɪɪŋ deɪ,
ənd tɒtʃ ðə stɒbəl-pleɪnz wɪð ɹouzɪ hjuɪ;
ðen ɪn ə weɪlfʊl kwaɪə ðə smɔɪl næts mɔɪn
əmɒŋ ðə ɹɪvə sælouz, bɔɪn əlɔft
ɔɪ sɪŋkɪŋ æz ðə laɪt waɪnd lɪvz ɔɪ daɪz;
ənd fʊl-gɹoun læmz laud bliɪt fɹəm hɪlɪ bɔɪn;
hedʒ-kɹɪkɪts sɪŋ; ənd nau wɪð tɹebəl sɔft
ðə ɹed-bɹɛst ʍɪsəlz fɹəm ə gaɪdn-kɹʋft;
ənd gæðɹɪŋ swɔlouz twɪtə ɪn ðə skaɪz.

12. ðə þɹʊsl.—baɪ tenɪsən.

sɒmə ɪz kɒmɪŋ, sɒmə ɪz kɒmɪŋ
aɪ nou ɪt, aɪ nou ɪt, aɪ nou ɪt,
laɪt əgeɪn, liːf əgeɪn, laɪf əgeɪn, lɒv əgeɪn,
jes maɪ waɪld lɪtl pouɪt.

sɪŋ ðə njuː jɪəɹ ɪn ɒndə ðə bluː
laɪst jɪə ju sæŋ ɪt əz glædlɪ
njuː, njuː, njuː, njuː! ɪz ɪt ðen sou njuː
ðət ju ʃʊd kæɹəl so mɪædlɪ?

lɒv əgeɪn, sɒŋ əgeɪn, nest əgeɪn, jɒŋ əgeɪn,
nevəɹ ə pɹɒfɪt sou kɹeɪzɪ,
ənd haɪdlɪ ə deɪzɪ əz jet lɪtl fɹend,
siː, ðəɹ ɪz haɪdlɪ ə deɪzɪ

hɪəɹ əgeɪn, hɪə, hɪə, hɪə, hæpɪ jɪə!
ou wɔːbl, ɒntʃɪdn, ɒnbɪdn!
sɒməɹ ɪz kɒmɪŋ, ɪz kɒmɪŋ, maɪ dɪə
ənd ɔːl ðə wɪntəz aɪ hɪdən

13 ɒn ðə pɹouz staɪl əv pouɪts —baɪ wɪljəm hæzlət

ɪt əz ɔːlweɪz əpɪəd tə miː ðət ðə moust pʌɹfɪkt pɹouz staɪl,
ðə moust pɑuəfʊl, ðə moust dæzlɪŋ, ðə moust dɛɹɪŋ, ðæt
ʍɪtʃ went ðə nɪəɹəst tə ðə vʌɪdʒ əv pouɪtɹɪ, ənd jet nevə
fel ouvə. wəz bʌɪks. ɪt hæz ðə sɒlɪdɪtɪ ənd spaɪklɪŋ ɪfekt
əv ðə daɪəmənd· ɔːl ɒðə fain ɹaɪtɪŋ ɪz laɪk fɹenʃ peɪst ɔɪ
bɹɪstəl-stounz ɪn ðə kəmpæɹɪzn. bʌɪks staɪl ɪz ɛəɹ, flaɪtɪ,
ədventʃəɹəs, bɒt ɪt nevə luɪzɪz saɪt əv ðə sɒbdjɪkt, neɪ, ɪz
ɔːlweɪz ɪn kɒntækt wɪð, ənd dɹɹaɪvz ɪts ɪnkɹɪst ɔɪ vɛɹɪŋ
ɪmpɒls fɹʌm ɪt. ·ɪt meɪ bɪ sed tə paɪs jɔɪnɪŋ gɒlfs 'ɒn ði
ɒnstedfast fʊtɪŋ əv ə spɪə'; stɪl ɪt hæz ən æktjuəl ɹestɪŋ-
pleɪs ənd tænʒəbl səpɔɪt ɒndəɹ ɪt—ɪt ɪz nɒt səspendɪd ɒn
nɒþɪŋ. ɪt dɪfəɹ fɹəm pouɪtɹɪ, æz aɪ kənsiːv, laɪk ðə ʃamwɑ

fɹəm ði iːgl, it klaimz tu ən ɔːlmoust iːkwəl hait, tɒtʃiz əpɒn ə klɑud, ouvəluks ə pɹesipis, iz piktʃəɹesk, səblaim— bɒt, ɔːl ðə ʍail, insted əv sɔːɹiŋ þɹu ði ɛə, it stændz əpɒn ə ɹʊki kliːf, klæmbəz ʊp bai əbɹɒpt ənd intɹiːkit weiz, ənd bɹɑuziz ɒn ðə ɹɒfəst bɑːk, ɔː kɹɒps ðə tendə flɑuə. ðə pɹinsəpl ʍitʃ gaidz hiz pen iz tɹuːþ, nɒt bjuːti—nɒt pleʒə, bɒt pɑuə.

. . . . . .

lɔid baiɹənz pɹouz iz bæd ; ðæt iz tə sei, hevi, leiˈbəd ənd kɔːs : hi tɹaiz tə nɒk sɒmwɒn dɑun wið ðə bɒt-end əv evɹi lain, ʍitʃ difiːts hiz ɒbdʒikt—ənd ðə stail əv ði ɔːþəɹ əv weivəli (if hi kɒmz fɛəli intu ðis diskɒʃən) æz miə stail iz vilənəs. it iz pɹiti plein hi iz ə pouit ; fə ðə sɑund əv neimz ɹɒnz məkænikəli in hiz iəz, ənd hi ɹiŋz ðə tʃeindʒiz ɒnkɒnʃəsli ɒn ðə seim wʌɹdz in ə sentəns, laik ðə seim ɹaimz in ə kɒplət.

nɒt tə spin ɑut ðis diskɒʃən tu mɒtʃ, ai wud kənkluːd bai əbsʌːviŋ, ðət sɒm əv ði ould iŋgliʃ pɹouz-ɹaitəz (hu wə nɒt pouits) ɑː ðə best, ənd, ət ðə seim taim, ðə moust pouetikl in ðə feivəɹəbl sens. əmɒŋ ðiːz wi mei ɹekn sɒm əv ði ould divainz, ən dʒeɹəmi teilə ət ðə hed əv ðem. ðeɹ iz ə flɒʃ laik ðə dɒn ouvə hiz ɹaitiŋz, ðə swiːtnəs əv ðə ɹouz, ðə fɹeʃnəs əv ðə mɔːniŋ djuː, ðeɹ iz ə sɒftnəs in hiz stail, pɹəsiːdiŋ fɹəm ðə tendənəs əv hiz hɑːt : bət hiz hed iz fʌːm, ənd hiz hænd iz fɹiː. hiz motiɹiəlz ɑːɹ əz fainli ɹɔːt ʊp əz ðei ɑːɹ əɹidʒinəl ənd ətɹæktif in ðəmselvz. miltənz pɹouz-stail seivəz tu mɒtʃ əv pouitɹi, ənd, əz ai əv ɔːlɹedi hintid, əv ən imiteiʃn əv ðə lætin. dɹaidnz iz pʌɹfiktli ɒneksepʃnəl, ənd ə mɒdəl, in simplisiti, stɹeŋþ ənd pʌːspikjuːiti, fə ðə sɒbdʒikts hi tɹiːtid ɒv.

14. fɹəm ‘ði ould kjuːɹiɒsiti ʃɒp.’

‘ðis iz ðə pleis,’ hi sed, pɔːsiŋ ət ə dɔː tə put nel dɑun ən teik hʌ hænd, ‘dount bi əfɹeid, ðɛəz noubədi hiə wil hɑːm ju.’

it niːdɪd ə stɹʌŋ kɔnfɪdəns *in* ðɪs əʃuɹəns tʊ *i* nduːs ðəm
tu entə, ənd ʍɔt ðeɪ sɔː ɪnsaɪd dɪd nɔt dɪmɪnɪʃ ðeəɹ æpɹɪ'henʃn
ənd əlɑːm   *in* ə lɑːdʒ ənd lᵊfti bɪldɪŋ, səpɔɪtɪd baɪ pɪləz
əv aɪən, wɪð gɹeɪt blæk æpətʃəz *in* ðɪ ɒpə wɔːlz, oupn tə
ðɪ *i*kstɑːnl ɛə ; ᵊkouɪŋ tə ðə ɹuːf wɪð ðə biːtɪŋ əv hæməz
ənd ɹɔɪ əv fʌɪnəsɪz, mɪŋgəld wɪð ðə hɪsɪŋ əv ɹed-hɔt metəl
plɒndʒd *in* wɔːtə, ənd ə hɒndɹəd stɹeɪndʒ ɒnɑːþlɪ nɔɪzɪz
nevə hɑːd elsʍɛə ; ɪn ðɪs gluːmɪ pleɪs, muːvɪŋ laɪk diːmənz
əmɒŋ ðə fleɪm ənd smouk, dɪmlɪ ənd fɪtfʊlɪ siːn, flɒʃt ən
tɔːmentɪd baɪ ðə bʌɪnɪŋ faɪəz, ənd wiːldɪŋ gɹet wepɒnz, ə
fɔːltɪ blou fɹəm enɪ wɒn əv ʍɪtʃ mɒst əv kɹɒʃt sɒm wʌɪkmənz
skɒl, ə nɒmbəɹ əv men leɪbəd laɪk dʒaɪənts ; ɒðəz ɹɪpousɪŋ
əpɒn hiːps əv koul ɔɪ æʃɪz, wɪð ðɛə feɪsɪz tʌɪnd tə ðə blæk vɔɪlt
əbɒv, slept ɔ ɹestɪd fɹəm ðɛə tɔɪl, ɒðəz əgeɪn, oupnɪŋ ðə
ʍaɪt-hɔt fʌɪnɪs-dɔːz, kɑːst fjuːəl ɔn ðə fleɪmz, ʍɪtʃ keɪm
ɹɒʃɪŋ ənd ɹɔːɹɪŋ fɔɪþ tə miːt ɪt, ənd lɪkt ɪt ɒp laɪk ɔɪl.
ɒðəz dɹuː fɔɪþ, wɪð klæʃɪŋ nɔɪz, əpɒn ðə gɹaʊnd, gɹeɪt ʃiːts
əv glouɪŋ stiːl, ɪmɪtɪŋ ən *i*nsəpɔɪtəbl hiːt, ənd ə dɒl diːp
laɪt laɪk ðæt ʍɪtʃ redənz *in* ðɪ aɪz əv sævɪdʒ biːsts þɹuː
ðiːz bɪwɪldɹɪŋ saɪts ənd defnɪŋ saʊndz, ðɛə kəndɒktə led
ðəm tu ʍɛə, ɪn ə dɑːk pɔːʃn əv ðə bɪldɪŋ, wɒn fʌɪnɪs bʌɪnt
baɪ naɪt ən deɪ—sou, ət liːst, ðeɪ gæðəd fɹəm ðə mouʃən
əv·ɪz lɪps, fəɹ əz jet ðeɪ kʊd ounlɪ siː hɪm spɪːk : nɔt hɪə
hɪm. ðə mæn huː hæd biːn wɔːtʃɪŋ ðɪs faɪə, ənd huɪz tɑːsk
wəz endɪd fə ðə pɹezənt, glædlɪ wɪðdɹuː, ənd left ðəm wɪð
ðɛə fɹend, huː, spɹedɪŋ nelz lɪtl klouk əpɒn ə hiːp əv æʃɪz,
ənd ʃouɪŋ hʌː ʍɛə ʃɪ kʊd hæŋ həɹ ɑːtə klouðz tə dɹaɪ, saɪnd
tə hʌː ənd ðɪ ould mæn tə laɪ daʊn ənd sliːp. fəɹ *i*mself,
hɪ tʊk hɪz steɪʃn ɔn ə ɹæɡɪd mæt bɪfɒ ðə fʌɪnɪs-dɔɪ, ənd
ɹestɪŋ hɪz tʃɪn əpɒn hɪz hændz, wɔtʃt ðə fleɪm əz ɪt ʃɒn þɹuː
ðɪ aɪən tʃɪŋks, ən ðə ʍaɪt æʃɪz əz ðeɪ fel *i*ntu ðɛə bɹaɪt, hɔt
gɹeɪv bɪlou.

15. fɹəm beɪknz esɪ 'əv gɑːdnz.'

gᴐd ɔːlmaɪti fʌːst plɑːntɪd ə gɑːdn, ənd ɪndiːd ɪt ɪz ðə
pjuːɹəst əv hjuːmən pleʒɔz.   ɪt ɪz ðə gɹeɪtəst ɹɪfɹeʃmənt tə
ðə spɪɹɪts əv mæn ; wɪðaʊt ʍɪtʃ, bɪldɪŋz ənd pæləsɪz ɑː bt
gɹous hændɪ·wʌːks. . . . aɪ du hould ɪt, ɪn ðə rᴐɪjəl ɔɪdəɹɪŋ
əv gɑːdnz, ðɛɑɹ ɔːt tə bɪ gɑːdnz fər ɔːl mɒnþs ɪn ðə jɪə, ɪn
ʍɪtʃ sevɹəlɪ þɪŋz əv bjuːtɪ meɪ bɪ ðen ɪn siːzn, . . . ənd
bɪkɔz ðə bɹeþ əv flaʊəz ɪz fɑː swiːtəɹ ɪn ðɪ ɛə (ʍɛɑɹ ɪt kɒmz
ən(d) gouz, laɪk ðə wɑːblɪŋ əv mjuːzɪk) ðn ɪn ðə hænd,
ðɛəfᴐː nɒþɪŋ ɪz mᴐɪ fɪt ʃɔ ðæt dɪlaɪt, ðn tə nou ʍᴐt bi ðə
flaʊəz, ənd plɑːnts, ðt du bɛst pʌfjuːm ðɪ ɛə. . . . ʃɔ
gɑːdnz (spiːkɪŋ əv ðouz ʍɪtʃ ɑːɹ ɪndiːd pɹɪns-laɪk, əz wi əv
dɒn əv bɪldɪŋz) ðə kᴐntents ɔːt nᴐt wel tə bɪ ɒndə þʌːtɪ eɪkəz
əv gɹaʊnd, ənd tə bɪ dɪvaɪdɪd ɪntu þɹiː pɑːts : ə gɹiːn ɪn
ðɪ entɹəns, ə hiːþ ɔ dezʌːt ɪn ðə gouɪŋ fɔːþ, ənd ðə meɪn
gɑːdn ɪn ðə mɪdst, bɪsaɪdz ælɪz, ᴐn bouþ saɪdz.

ðə gɹiːn hæþ tuː pleʒəz ; ðə won, bɪkᴐz nɒþɪŋ ɪz mᴐɪ plezənt
tə ðɪ aɪ ðn gɹiːn gɹɑːs kept faɪnlɪ ʃᴐːn ; ðɪ ɒðə, bɪkᴐz ɪt wɪl
gɪv ju ə fɛɑɹ ælɪ ɪn ðə mɪdst baɪ ʍɪtʃ ju meɪ gou ɪn fɹɒnt
əpᴐn ᴐ steɪtlɪ hedʒ, ʍɪtʃ ɪz tu ɪnkɹouz ðə gɑːdn.   bɒt bɪkᴐz
ðɪ ælɪ wɪl bɪ lɒŋ. ənd, ɪn gɹeɪt hiːt əv ðə jɪə ᴐ deɪ, ju ɔːt
nᴐt tu baɪ ðə ʃeɪd ɪn ðə gɑːdn, baɪ gouɪŋ ɪn ðə son þɹuː ðə
gɹiːn, ðɛəfᴐː ju ɑː, əv iːðə saɪd ðə gɹiːn, tə plɑːnt ə kɒvə ælɪ,
əpᴐn kɑːpəntəz wʌːk, əbaʊt twelv fʊt ɪn haɪt, baɪ ʍɪtʃ ju
meɪ gou ɪn ʃeɪd, ɪntu ðə gɑːdn.

GLASGOW : PRINTED AT THE UNIVERSITY PRESS BY ROBERT MACLEHOSE AND CO. LTD.

9 781018 549347